What's that Tree?

For my grandchildren: Joshua, Cael, Grace and Kelsea – conservation is their future, and it is my hope that an appreciation of biodiversity can start with their love of knowing trees.

Published by Struik Nature
(an imprint of Random House Struik (Pty) Ltd)
80 McKenzie Street, Cape Town, 8001
PO Box 1144, Cape Town, 8000 South Africa

Company Reg. No. 1966/003153/07

Visit us at **www.randomstruik.co.za**
Log on to our photographic website **www.imagesofafrica.co.za**
for an African experience.

First published 2011
1 3 5 7 9 10 8 6 4 2

Publisher: **Pippa Parker**
Managing editor: **Helen de Villiers**
Editor: **Emily Bowles**
Designer: **Dominic Robson**
Proofreader: **Tessa Kennedy**

Reproduction by Hirt & Carter Cape (Pty) Ltd
Printed and bound by Tien Wah Press (Pte) Limited, Singapore

ISBN 978 1 77007 831 4

Front cover (top): Burke's fig (*Ficus burkei*) (Photo: CV)
Front cover (bottom): Quiver-tree aloe (*Aloe dichotoma*) (Photo: AG)
Page 1: Wonderboom fig (*Ficus salicifolia* spp.) (Photo: JB);
Page 2: *Erythrina lysistemon* (Photo: JB); **Page 4:** African dog-rose (*Xylotheca kraussiana*) flower (Photo: GG); **Page 5 (top):** Ana tree (*Faidherbia albida*) pod. **Page 5 (bottom):** Smelly-berry fingerleaf (*Vitex mombasse*) (Photo: BW).

A word from the author

Being able to identify trees in southern Africa is exciting and rewarding. More and more tree books have become available to assist the enthusiast – ranging from those that are comprehensive, to those with a focus on the trees of a particular genus or region. However, up until now there has been a dearth of books that provide a simple entry point for the novice. This latest addition to Struik Nature's *What's that?* series will, I hope, help to bridge that gap.

This volume details ~500 species out of a regional total of ~1 700 species. Meg Coates Palgrave's *Trees of Southern Africa*, revised and updated in 2002, is, to my mind, the best and most comprehensive text of its kind and full accounts of all the species that I deal with here can be found in that tome. The recognition and identification of such a large number of tree species can be daunting, even for an expert. My aim is to assist you to navigate your way to as many of the most common and conspicuous tree families and genera as possible, before you try to identify trees at the species level. The advantage of this approach is that rather than becoming bogged down in a sea of botanical terminology and a mass of detailed photography, you can focus on just a few key features for a group. Useful hints are also given to help you identify the more problematic families and species.

Building up a 'search image' for a particular tree family and then for individual species is critical. For example, many tree genera have a distinctive growth form. Spectacular examples are aloes, cycads, palms, tree-ferns, wild bananas and cabbage-trees, which are easy to recognise at genus level. At the species level many trees are readily identified if you know to look out for a few simple features. One problem that tree spotters frequently encounter is that some species are highly variable vegetatively. If you understand and are prepared for that variability then identification also becomes easier.

Getting to know what distinguishes a genus and fleshing out your search image with a detailed knowledge of individual species requires a reasonable memory and some practice. Once you recognise how a tree differs from those around it or from those that you already know, you're halfway there. The challenge is to identify unknown species by searching for their unique characteristics. The more trees you know, the easier it becomes, and the more enjoyable and satisfying.

I have tried to use plain English wherever possible. Plants are given scientific names according to strict conventions, but this is not the case with common names. Trees often have one common name in one region and another elsewhere. Also, authors of different tree books may choose to use their preferred common names. There is, therefore, an urgent need to standardise the common names used. In this book I have tried to base common names on their taxonomic binomials. Ideally, we need an international body to take on the task of formulating rules for common names so that, in time, they can be standardised globally.

Finally, the arrangement of families in this tree book differs from the more familiar arrangement. Tree guides traditionally follow a classification system devised in the early 1900s and based on the interpretations of Engler and Prantl. Recent DNA studies have suggested a somewhat different classification and I have chosen to use this updated arrangement, which is known as Angiosperm Phylogeny Group, 2nd revision, or APGII.

So take your time, enjoy, and keep growing your personal tree life-list.

Eugene Moll

Contents

Introduction

Learning to identify southern Africa's trees presents a considerable challenge, since the region is home to approximately 1 700 different species, both indigenous and introduced. This book is designed to make the beginner's task much easier, by introducing trees in family groups. Placing them within the context of their family is useful: although a few trees defy family relationship 'rules' and appear entirely different from their closest relatives, most related species do, fortunately, exhibit similar vegetative characteristics.

Each family group features species that are eye-catching, widespread, unusual or interesting in some way. Among them are trees that:

- are conspicuous along the highways and byways of southern Africa
- may catch your eye when you are walking to the beach or through the bush
- have a particular, easily recognisable growth form or shape that may attract your attention
- are seasonally spectacular from afar because of the flowers, fruits or leaves
- have specific characteristics that are diagnostic from close-up such as distinctive bark, round woody fruits, large spines or wonderfully scented flowers
- are aromatic, hairy, or have hooked spines that seize your clothing when you brush past.

To give you some idea of how many species there are in each family, the global and regional number of member species (based largely on the 3rd edition of *Trees of Southern Africa* by Meg Coates Palgrave) is listed at the beginning of the family account. Thus, if you come across a tree that does not match those illustrated, the chances are that it is one of those excluded and, to find its name, you will need to search elsewhere in the literature.

There are two exceptions to the rule of grouping trees by family. The first group discussed in this book comprises trees that are characteristic of a highly specialised habitat – namely estuaries and coastal lagoons (page 16). The other (page 126) groups together dwarf species from four different families that all resemble African baobabs. The remaining group entries in the book present tree families according to their evolutionary sequence, starting with ferns, moving on to cone-bearing plants and then, finally, to flowering plants.

The **Kaoko sesame-bush** has an easily recognisable growth form.

What is a tree?

Most people agree that trees are large, woody plants. However, there is no absolute scientific definition of a tree, simply because woody plants vary considerably, not just in size and shape but also in the woodiness of their trunks.

For the purposes of this book, trees are defined as free-standing, woody plants that generally reach a height of 3–4 m and have a girth at chest height of at least 100 mm. Some smaller species have also been included, such as those that appear to be significant woody plants in the arid west and in the mountains of the south, where 'real' trees are few and far between.

The **Camel thorn** (*Acacia erioloba*) is a member of the Fabaceae or legume family.

WHAT IS A FAMILY?

Taxonomy is the science of classifying living things into a hierarchy, following various criteria. At the lowest level of this hierarchy are individual species. They are grouped together into genera. All species have a binomial (double-barrelled) scientific name, usually with a Latin or Greek derivation. The first name indicates to which genus an individual belongs; the second identifies the particular species. Above the genus level in the hierarchy is the family, or occasionally the subfamily. In this book we've dealt with just one family that incorporates subfamilies, namely the Legumes (Fabaceae). For example, the Camel thorn family tree looks like this:

Family: Legume family (Fabaceae)
Subfamily: Thorn trees (Mimosoideae)
Genus: Thorn trees (*Acacia*)
Species: Camel thorn (*A. erioloba*)

Scientists are constrained by a strict body of rules when they choose a scientific name for a species. However, this is not the case with common names, which can vary greatly according to language, area or custom. Because common names are often more familiar and easier for beginners to use, they are given along with scientific names in this book (generally following those in the *SAPPI Tree Spotter's Life List*).

What to look for when identifying trees

Most people can already identify some trees, such as the following:

- flowering giants like jacarandas (*Jacaranda mimosifolia*)
- ornamentals like palms (e.g. *Livingstonia* spp.), aloes (*Aloe* spp.) and tibouchinas (*Tibouchina* spp.)
- timber plantation species like pines (*Pinus* spp.), wattles (*Acacia* spp.) and gums (*Eucalyptus* spp.)
- iconic indigenous trees, such as the African marula (*Sclerocarya birrea*), the African baobab (*Adansonia digitata*), the proteas (*Protea* spp.) or the iconic flat-topped *Acacia* thorn trees

These trees all have distinctive features – canopy shape, trunk characteristics, leaves, flowers or fruits – that reveal their identity. However, not all trees provide such handy clues. Less easily identifiable species require that you first familiarise yourself with the different parts that make up the tree and then note the characteristics of these parts. Some trees are particularly tricky to identify because not all parts are visible all of the time: a specimen may be easy to identify when in flower or in fruit, but outside of this season the clues to its identity may lie in its leaves, bark or stature. In some cases these vegetative characteristics are rather variable and therefore not very useful.

The best way of getting to know about trees is to learn the names of those that you regularly see, and to take note of their unique features. Consider why you are able to recognise a particular species. What, on reflection, are its distinguishing characteristics? What is the 'search image' you have constructed for that species that helps you to recognise it when you see it?

Basic architecture

To identify a tree begin by considering its size and shape. Does it have a single, straight, unbranched trunk, a crooked trunk or many stems that branch from the base? What is the arrangement of the branches and leaves? Does the canopy have a distinctive shape? Different combinations of trunks and leaves may help you to identify a species. For instance, palms may have a straight single trunk topped by an apical bunch of fibrous leaves. Aloes have a similar growth form to that of palms, but differ in that their leaves are succulent and they bear bright flowers in winter. By contrast, strelitzias (*Strelitzia* spp.), which also have simple straight trunks, have large flat leaves that become wind-shredded with age.

Note that not all trees of the same species have the same shape – they can differ vastly in form depending on the age of the individual and the environment in which it is growing.

In this book we define *large trees* as those with an upright unbranched trunk of >0.5 m in diameter and that are at least 6 m tall, mostly with a large spreading canopy. *Small trees* are those that are ~3 m tall, some with a well-developed canopy and usually with many stems. (Some aloes have small canopies and single stems and are included here.) *Medium trees* fall in between these extremes, and can be multi-stemmed or branch low down. They usually have crooked trunks. Size is strongly influenced by where trees grow: species that are small in harsh environments may grow quite large where the soil or climate is more suitable.

Palms typically have a single straight trunk topped by an apical bunch of fibrous leaves.

Deciduous or evergreen

Most trees get their energy from photosynthesis, the process by which leaves use sunlight to convert carbon dioxide and water into sugars. While sunlight and carbon dioxide are generally abundant, water is often limited. When water is scarce, photosynthesis must either cease or be severely curtailed. Trees do this in various ways: they may greatly reduce the leaf surface area by being deciduous, i.e. by dropping their leaves in the dry season, or they may have evolved structural adaptations to minimise water loss.

Many plants in southern Africa have structural adaptations for coping with arid conditions, including:

- succulent vegetative parts for storing water, e.g. the trunk of the African baobab, the twigs of euphorbias (*Euphorbia* spp.) or the leaves of aloes (*Aloe* spp.)
- reduced leaf surface area, e.g. the minute leaflets of the Grey camel-thorn (*Acacia haematoxylon*) or the very tiny and tightly rolled leaves of ericas (*Erica* spp.)
- extremely tough and leathery leaves like those of proteas (*Protea* spp.)
- hairy and even woolly leaves likes those of the Cape silver-tree (*Leucadendron argenteum*), Coastal silver-oaks (*Brachylaena discolor*) and the camphors (*Tarchonanthus* spp.)

To produce leaves trees need not only the carbohydrates produced by photosynthesis, but also nutrients like nitrogen, phosphorus and potassium, which are used for protein synthesis. In nutrient-poor environments reducing leaf surface area by being deciduous is not an option, because leaves are expensive to renew. Therefore, trees growing in nutrient-poor regions tend to be evergreen, and their leaves are well adapted to survive the tough conditions.

So, in the Western Cape, where soils are nutrient-poor, the predominant vegetation is fynbos, and it is evergreen. Similarly, the Magic guarri (*Euclea divinorum*) is evergreen: it grows on seasonally waterlogged sites in the lowveld, where the soils become anaerobic – depleted of oxygen – and the roots are unable to breathe and so cannot take up nutrients. Mangroves are also evergreen, as estuarine soils contain little oxygen.

Leaves

The size, shape, colour, texture and aroma of a tree's leaves all provide clues to the identity of the species. It is important to notice how the leaves are arranged on the twigs and whether they are simple or compound, and to look at structural features like the leaf base, apex and margins. The illustrated glossary on page 176 gives useful examples of the different leaf forms and features.

Regionally, leaf size, shape and texture vary considerably, and there is even some variation within individuals of the same species. Some plants have huge leaves (e.g. *Raphia* palms), others, like many lowveld trees, have smaller leaves, while still others have tiny scale-like leaves (e.g. *Widdringtonia* cedars). Consider the shape of the leaf: is it the simple flat leaf shape that is typical of most afromontane forest species, or is it perhaps strap-like or needle-like? Is it simply or more intricately divided like the leaves of a cabbage-tree (*Cussonia* spp.)? What sort of texture does it have? Is it pliable or brittle, soft or sandpapery, thin or thickly succulent? Similarly, you should note the coloration, which can range from shades of green and even grey, to yellows and reds depending on the time of year. Is the leaf surface glossy, dull or hairy? Some leaves give off a pleasant or unpleasant smell when crushed. A combination of these characteristics can aid you in building up a diagnostic description of a species.

Note the structural details of the leaf: this example has 3–5 veins running from its base, has serrate margins and tapers towards the apex.

Sap or gum

Sap or gum may be a key identifying characteristic. Members of some tree families, such as figs (*Ficus* spp.), produce copious milky sap that flows from the stem if a leaf is plucked. Others like members of the mango family (Anacardiaceae) exude clear and/or resinous sap or gum from injured trunks and branches.

Bark

A small percentage of trees are easily identified by their bark, e.g. the Leadwood bushwillow (*Combretum imberbe*) and the Paperbark albizia (*Albizia tanganyicensis*). Note whether the bark is smooth, rough or cracked, flaky or not, pale or darkly coloured.

Paperbark albizias have distinctive papery bark.

Robust spines on zigzagging twigs are a characteristic of **Camel thorns**.

The yellow male and pink female parts of **Bushveld sickle-bush** flowers are separate.

Spines

In our region many trees are spinescent and the colour, shape and texture of these spines and their distribution on the tree vary considerably. Most spiny trees occur in bushveld. They can also occur in many other vegetation types, but are rare in fynbos.

Flowers and fruits

If the species that you're trying to identify is in flower, note the size and colour of the flowers. Are they tiny and pale or large and showy? Are they short-lived, or do they persist for some time? Also note whether the flowers occur singly, close together in tight flower heads (inflorescences) like members of the daisy and protea families, or in lax flower heads like the Kei bottlebrush (*Greyia flanaganii*). Striking flowers generally make a tree more conspicuous and readily identifiable.

If the tree is bearing fruit, then are the fruits tiny or are they large like those of the African sausage-tree (*Kigelia africana*), which has fruits that weigh several kilograms? Are they dry or fleshy, or do they have a hard and persistent outer shell? Some fruits are toxic, so be cautious and don't eat them unless you are sure of the tree's identity and know that the fruit is edible.

Region or habitat

Tree habitat and distribution information can be a great aid to identification. The location of a tree determines its appearance and size to some extent. Because many trees, such as mangroves, are extremely habitat specific, species can often be identified by where they grow. Refer to the distribution given in the species accounts and to the vegetation and place name maps that follow.

Southern African map – political and physical

The vegetation types of southern Africa

Trees occur throughout most of southern Africa. The vegetation of the region has been divided into different types, each with its own distinctive species:

- forest
- fynbos
- karoo
- desert
- grassland
- bushveld
- mangroves and associated communities

The map below shows six of the seven major vegetation types. Some forest patches as well as the mangrove estuaries and lagoons along the coast north of East London are not mapped as they are too tiny at this scale.

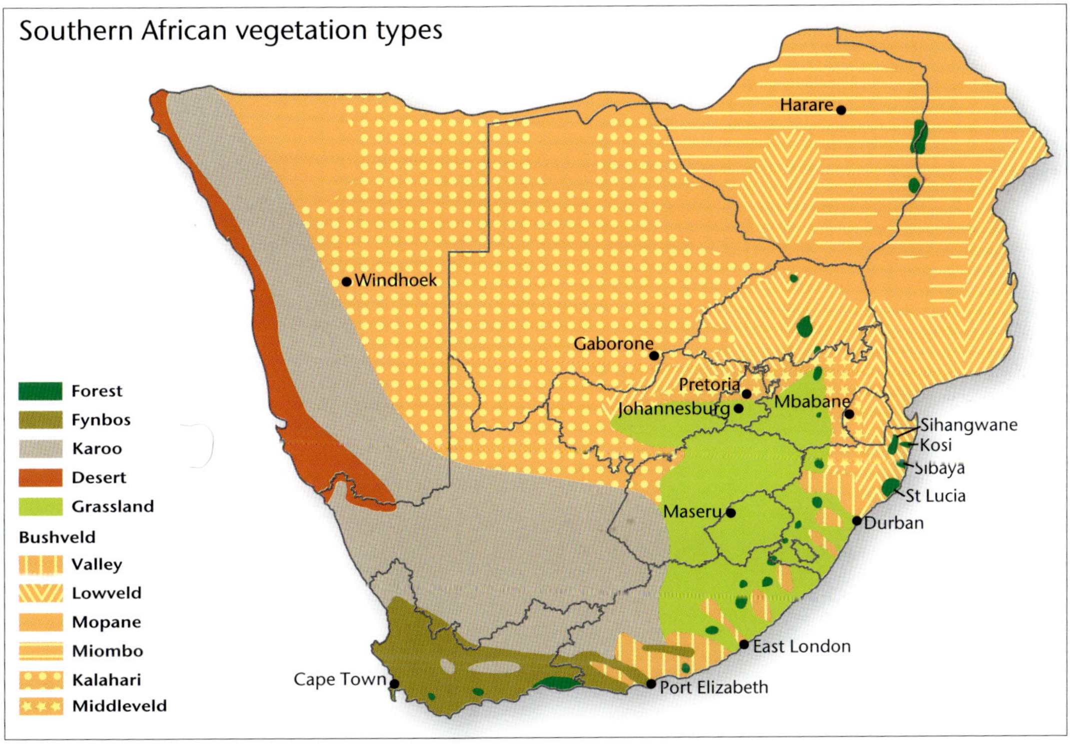

Forest

Forests are plant communities in which trees dominate. Generally the trees are large and evergreen, growing so close together that their canopies touch, creating an internal microclimate. Forest trees may be difficult to identify because they are so tall that their leaves, flowers and fruits are too high to be seen in detail. Generally, forests grow only where the rainfall is at least 1 000 mm per year, and where this moisture is supplemented by frequent mist. The main forest types in the region are the following:

Afromontane forest is the most common and widespread forest type in the region. Patches range in size from a hectare to the ~80 000 hectare block at Knysna/Tsitsikamma. These forests form a discontinuous chain from Cape Town eastwards along the coastal mountain ranges to Knysna, northeast to Port Elizabeth, and inland along the Drakensberg escarpment to the Soutpansberg and the Chimanimani Mountains in Zimbabwe. The further north, the greater the number of climbers and epiphytes and the taller and more tropical the trees.

Lowland (or coastal) forest varies from wet to dry types and occurs mainly on sandy soils on the coastal plain north of Richards Bay, and is also found at Alexandria and in KwaZulu-Natal at St Lucia, Lake Sibaya and Kosi Bay. Isolated patches of sand forest, a unique dry forest type, occur east of the Pongola River, into southern Mozambique and even in the extreme northern and eastern parts of the Kruger Park.

Many patches of **afromontane forest** occur in ravines and as isolated islands below cliffs.

Dune forest along the coast is often well pruned by wind shear as this canopy of White milkwoods illustrates.

A **sand forest** can have very large trees and an open canopy.

Dune forest, a low, tangled, impenetrable forest form, occurs on sandy substrates in a more or less continuous belt from Port Elizabeth to the Zambezi River.

Swamp forest is very limited in extent: remnants still occur north of Durban. These forests occur in seasonal freshwater swamps. The trees are generally tall and ferns are a common component.

Riparian forest and woodlands occur where conditions are suitable along most of the major rivers that flow into the Indian Ocean, and in the lower reaches of the Orange River. They form a narrow fringing band of open or closed patches of trees.

Fynbos

Fynbos is an evergreen, shrub-dominated vegetation type. Today only small trees occur in this region because of frequent burning and historical exploitation. Fynbos occurs in a roughly L-shaped block from north of Cape Town, eastwards to about Port Elizabeth. Small islands also occur on sandy soils in Pondoland, inland of Durban and in the Drakensberg Mountains, in the highlands of Mpumalanga and Limpopo, and finally on the Chimanimani Mountains of Zimbabwe. Fynbos is determined not by climate, but by soil nutrient status: while it can occur in the Mediterranean climate of the Western Cape, around Port Elizabeth where rainfall can occur year-round, and in the summer rainfall areas of the north, it is always confined to nutrient-poor, mostly sandy soils.

Typical **fynbos** is a mixture of flowering shrubby species with almost no trees.

The Little Karoo is characterised by **succulent karoo** vegetation. A few scattered Cape botterbooms can be seen in the foreground.

Note the scattered shrubs and the few annual grasses growing among the rocks in the arid environment of the northern Namib.

Karoo

Karoo vegetation comprises mostly tiny and widely scattered evergreen shrubs, although succulents are more common in the west. It occurs in the central and western regions, stretching north to the Cunene River. The climate is semi-arid and the few trees that do occur are small and are found mostly along drainage lines, including river banks, and sometimes on rocky outcrops.

Desert

With rainfall of <150 mm per year, plants struggle to survive in deserts. In our region desert occurs in the far northwest of South Africa, and up along the Namibian coast to Angola. Both sandy and stony deserts occur. Here trees and even large shrubs are extremely rare – and then only in rocky situations, on deep sands in the very north, and along drainage lines.

Grassland

A continuous cover of grasses and other herbaceous plants occurs on the central plateau of South Africa, which is known as the highveld, extending eastwards over the Drakensberg. These grasslands extend from about Queenstown as far north as Swaziland. Here trees are rare, except on rocky slopes and along drainage lines, although aliens and certain indigenous trees are becoming increasingly invasive.

A **grassland** winter scene east of the great escarpment showing the lack of trees and the snow on the Drakensberg.

Bushveld

Bushveld vegetation occupies some two-thirds of southern Africa – from Port Elizabeth northwards as far as Mpumalanga and westwards into Namibia. It is dominated chiefly by deciduous tree species and by numerous bushy species and has a highly variable grass and shrub understorey. The climate is strongly seasonal and, like grassland, bushveld is fire-prone. In the south the trees tend to be smaller, growing taller further east and towards the tropics. Bushveld covers a vast area and encompasses fairly moist to tropical climate in the east of South Africa, Mozambique and Zimbabwe and as far west as Caprivi in Namibia. In the western and central parts of the region the climate is drier, with very hot summers and freezing winter nights. Consequently, this is the most complex of all the vegetation types with trees. Over the ages it has been heavily impacted by people.

Typical **valley bushveld** in the Fish River Valley: the vegetation is conspicuously dense on the moister south-facing slope.

Bushveld mopanes make up a large proportion of the tree species in more arid **bushveld** areas. This large mopane on the edge of the Namib is in full fruit.

African marulas are significant **low-altitude bushveld** trees. They are a valuable resource both for people and for many animal species.

DP

Left: **Camel thorns** growing along a seasonal river in the Kalahari. ***Right:*** **Miombo bushveld** is renowned for the magnificent colours of the spring foliage. This vegetation dominates the old granitic soils through much of Zimbabwe.

Valley bushveld occurs along the east coast in areas where the terrain is deeply incised or undulating. In the south, inland of Port Elizabeth, it can be extremely dense and is known locally as Addo bush or succulent thicket. Succulents may be common in valley bushveld and many of the trees and bushes here are thorny and seasonally deciduous.

Lowveld (low-altitude) bushveld stretches from northern KwaZulu-Natal into the Limpopo River valley. Here the trees tend to be taller. On richer soils, Knob thorns (*Acacia nigrescens*) may dominate, while on lighter soils Bushwillows (*Combretum* spp.) and Cluster-leaves (*Terminalia* spp.) are common. Lowveld covers the Big Five country centred on the Kruger Park and extends eastwards into Mozambique. It has among the richest bushveld tree flora in Africa.

Mopane bushveld occurs in localised patches where Bushveld mopane (*Colophospermum mopane*) dominates. These sites are generally flat and sometimes seasonally waterlogged, with compact soils. Mopane bushveld is found on both shallow rocky and deeper sandy soils in the northern parts of South Africa, in the lowlands of Zimbabwe, and westwards into northern Botswana and Namibia.

Miombo or msasa bushveld is the dominant vegetation type on granitic soils in Zimbabwe and central Mozambique. Here the trees are large. They may form open or fairly closed communities.

Kalahari bushveld occurs mostly on sandy terrain, where there are occasional outcrops of calcium-rich soils, from central Botswana westwards and southwards into Namibia and northern South Africa. This vegetation type comprises open, rolling, grass-covered dunes with trees scattered mainly in the valleys.

Middleveld extends in an arc south of the Limpopo River to Mahikeng and Kimberley, and lies between the lowveld and the highveld grasslands. Generally trees are more widely scattered here than in the lowveld.

Mangroves and associated communities

Mangrove habitat is saline woodland or shrubland found in coastal environments, where fine sediments collect in areas protected from wave action. Plant species here have adapted to tolerate water that may range from brackish to pure seawater, to water that is twice as saline as the ocean.

Below: The **middleveld** is characterised by scattered Paper-bark thorns. Trees are far more scattered here than in the lowveld.

Mangroves & allied species

5 mangroves, the Lagoon hibiscus and the Powder-puff tree

CV

A typical young **White mangrove** with pencil roots.

The trees in this group do not constitute a family, but have been grouped together because they all live in very restricted and specialised habitats. As a result, they are more likely to be identified on account of their habitat than because of common morphological traits:

✓ all live in estuarine, lagoon and/or coastal lake habitats

From Port Elizabeth to Beira there are many lagoons, coastal lakes and/or estuaries that may be saline, or more or less fresh, depending on the tide and season. Very few tree species are able to grow in these specialised habitats. Those that do occur mostly grow colonially, forming fringes along banks, and they play a vital role in bank stabilisation in these hostile environments.

From north of East London the pencil roots of the **White mangrove** (*Avicennia marina*) are immediately diagnostic, and the leaves are bicoloured. **Black** (*Bruguiera gymnorrhiza*) and **Red** (*Rhizophora mucronata*) **mangroves**, with their shiny leaves, cigar-shaped fruits and their knee- and prop-roots, respectively, start to occur further north.

The most widespread, and arguably the most common, tree in this group is the small to medium-

AS

A small **Black mangrove** (*left*) growing alongside a **White mangrove** (*right*).

HFG

This image of a **Black mangrove** clearly illustrates the diagnostic knee-roots.

CV

White mangrove pencil roots forming a typical stubble on sandflats.

sized **Lagoon hibiscus** (*Hibiscus tiliaceus*); it has tangled branches and bright yellow flowers that soon turn orange and then reddish with age.

From north of Port Shepstone, mostly in the fresher backwaters of estuaries and lagoons, the magnificent medium-sized **Powder-puff tree** (*Barringtonia racemosa*) grows. It has pendent inflorescences~600 mm long, with widely separated tennis ball-sized flowers that open at night and soon fall off, drifting away on the current.

Today these habitats are greatly disturbed, and many of these trees no longer occur in profusion, if at all.

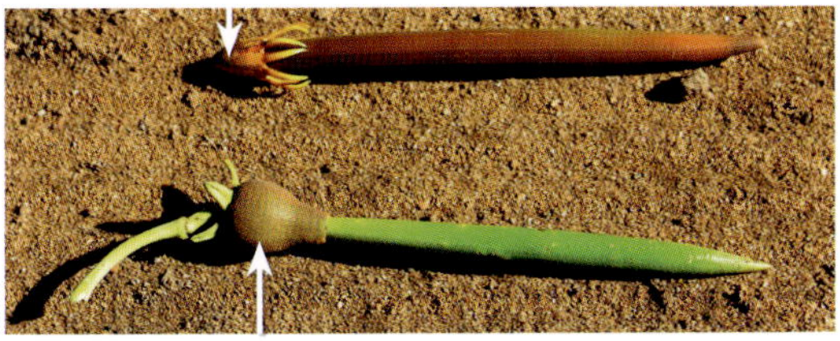
HFG

Fruits of the **Black (*top*)** and **Red (*bottom*) mangroves** showing the difference in the shape and structure of the persistent calyx.

TC

Red mangroves are easily identified by their spotted leaves and by the extension of the leaf's mid-vein – known as a 'mucro'.

The characteristic prop-roots of the **Red mangrove** silhouetted in a still lagoon.

TC

BP

The tennis ball-sized flowers of a **Powder-puff tree**.

BP

Lagoon hibiscus leaf: note its characteristic colour and texture.

EP

Lagoon hibiscus with a freshly opened yellow flower and an older orange flower. Note the greyish backs to the leaves.

Notes

- Mangrove swamps are tidal mud- and sand-flats where waterlogging depletes the soil of oxygen. If one digs down into the sludge this can release hydrogen sulphide (bad-egg gas), which is toxic, especially in confined spaces.
- Mangrove areas and lagoons are renowned as nurseries for young fish, which eventually go out to sea to complete their life cycles.
- The Kosi Estuary, with its associated mangrove communities and the chain of lakes to the south, is the only South African system still in a fairly pristine condition (see also section on habitats and the vegetation map of the region on p. 11).

Tree-fern Family

Cyatheaceae

~1 000 spp. globally; 4 spp. regionally, all trees

NC

The base of a **Forest tree-fern** showing the young green aphloeba (branched hair-like structures).

Striking plants that are easily recognised by their single stem and tight apical rosette of very large, soft-looking leaves:

- ✓ leaves uncoil as they expand
- ✓ leaves are much divided
- ✓ trunks are dark and very fibrous

All tree ferns occur in high-rainfall areas.

The **Forest tree-fern** (*Cyathea capensis*), as the name implies, grows in the forest subcanopy. A stream-bank specialist, it is ~5 m tall with leaves 2–3 m long. It can be identified by a tangled mass of green hair-like structures (known as aphloeba) at the leaf base, which later turn brown. It occurs from the Western Cape northwards into Africa.

The **Grassland tree-fern** (*C. dregei*) is a small tree to 3–5 m, with leaves up to 3 m long. It is most common on stream banks in mountain grassland, but can also occur on forest margins in rocky sites.

The last two tree-fern species, namely the **Spiny tree-fern** (*C. manniana*) and **Thomson's tree-fern** (*C. thomsonii*), occur only in the eastern highlands of Zimbabwe, in forest or on forest edges.

RB (main pic)

Grassland tree-ferns growing along a stream course. ***Inset:*** Spore-containing envelopes (sori) on the under-surface of the leaflets.

The characteristically coiled young leaf (frond) of a **Grassland tree-fern**.

BW (incl. inset)

A **Spiny tree-fern** in a forest environment. ***Inset:*** This tree-fern gets its name from the spines on its trunk.

Notes

- Ferns reproduce from spores, often contained in specialised envelopes (sori) on the under-surface of the leaves or fronds, as they are called in ferns.
- Although not deeply 'rooted', tree-ferns are not easily transplanted.

Cycad Family

Zamiaceae

~150 spp. globally; ~40 spp. regionally, ~35 spp. of tree

Cycads are easily identified by the following characters:

✓ leaves in a tight apical rosette
✓ leaflets very tough and thick, often spiky
✓ new fronds grow in an upright ring and then fold back with age
✓ large, pineapple-like cones, separate male and female, are produced on different plants
✓ very stout stems, which are bare and crisscrossed by leaf scars

JD (incl. inset)

▲ **Modjadji cycads** are the region's tallest cycads. ***Inset:*** Developing cones form in apical clusters.

Generally, these tropical and subtropical trees occur in bushveld or on forest margins, growing in localised groves. They are mostly found in rocky, low, mountainous sites in the eastern regions. The majority of cycads are hardly trees, and the few species that do get to tree size include:

The **Modjadji cycad** (*Encephalartos transvenosus*) in northern Limpopo is the most famous and tallest of the species (up to 13 m).

Two other large species, the **Giant cycad** (*E. natalensis*) and the **Eastern Cape giant cycad** (*E. altensteinii*), are similar looking; both rarely grow to 4–5 m.

Wood's cycad (*E. woodii*), from the Ongoye forest area, is now extinct in the wild, and only male plants survive in cultivation. They have an apical rosette of leaves that forms a spherical canopy.

Eastern Cape giant cycads with multiple heads. ***Inset:*** Ripe female cone: the bright red seeds are characteristic of cycads. ▼

JB

▲ A **Wood's cycad** growing in the Durban Botanic Gardens.

Notes

- Wild cycad populations are all strictly protected.
- Many cycads have been stolen from the wild and are even from gardens because they are valuable collectors' items. Unfortunately, they are easy to transplant.

Yellowwood Family

Podocarpaceae ~150 spp. globally; 4 spp. regionally, all trees

Six-year-old resprouting shoots on a **Breede river yellowwood** that was toppled in a gale.

Broad-leaved yellowwood fruits (1) showing attachment to the foot (2). Note the broad strap-like leaves with entire margins.

Close-up of a **Broad-leaved yellowwood** showing the characteristic stem ribbing (1) and the slightly twisted petiole (2).

Yellowwoods are mostly large, evergreen, forest trees. Male and female reproductive organs occur on different trees, and pollination is by wind. The fruits are roundish and bird/bat dispersed. Three species have their seeds attached to a fleshy 'foot', which is an additional dispersal morsel. These trees are easily recognisable by a combination of the characteristics that follow:

- ✓ leaves are simple, alternate and/or spirally arranged and often loosely clustered apically
- ✓ leaves are stiff and strap-shaped and much longer than they are wide
- ✓ young leaves (and fruit) can be covered in a bluish, powdery bloom that is easily wiped off
- ✓ margins entire and only the mid-vein is visible

The **Breede river yellowwood** (*Podocarpus elongatus*) is the only non-forest species and is confined to riparian and rocky communities in fynbos in the southwestern Cape. This tree grows in habitats that are episodically disturbed, and is the only species that re-sprouts. The canopy is spreading and can be very dense in old well-established individuals, reaching a maximum height of only ~6 m.

The **Broad-leaved yellowwood** (*P. latifolius*) is the most common and widespread species, and often occurs on forest edges and in rocky places close to forest. The young, bluish, short, straight and generally upright sun-leaves are tightly packed on twig ends (hence another common name, the Upright yellowwood). The exposed twigs can be festooned with the Old-man's-beard lichen and epiphytic orchids.

In shade the leaves of the **Broad-leaved yellowwood** may be much longer and can tend to droop a little. This may result in its being confused with the Drooping-leaved yellowwood.

The **Small-leaved yellowwood** (*Afrocarpus falcatus*) is sometimes also called the Outeniqua yellowwood because it is common in the Knysna forest. This forest tree has slightly sickle-shaped leaves that can be scattered along the twigs. This is arguably the tallest tree in South Africa, reaching heights of ~30 m. Small-leaved yellowwoods occur in many forest types, even in the swamp forests of coastal KwaZulu-Natal, although they are most common in afromontane forest along the escarpment.

The last of the four species is the **Drooping-leaved yellowwood** (*P. henkelii*), sometimes also known as Henkel's yellowwood. As the name implies, its leaves are much longer than those of other yellowwoods (100–150 mm, compared with 25–50 mm) and characteristically hang down. Like the Breede River yellowwood, this is a South African endemic. It occurs only in afromontane forests along the Great Escarpment, from about King William's Town to Pietermaritzburg.

A large **Drooping-leaved yellowwood**, which can emerge above the forest canopy. ***Inset:*** This close-up of the leaves shows their distinctive length and drooping habit.

A **Small-leaved yellowwood** with ripe fruit. Note that the seeds of this species lack a foot.

INTRODUCED SPECIES: Pines belong to the northern hemisphere Pinaceae family. Many species have commercial value and some have been introduced to South Africa. The Pinaceae is the largest conifer family with ~250 species and, like the Cupressaceae, is in the order Pinales. Pines are gymnosperms.

Local species that have become invasive in the summer rainfall area include *Pinus elliotii* and *P. patula*, and in the winter rainfall area, *P. radiata* and *P. pinaster*.

The genus *Pinus* is typified by having large, woody female cones and needle 'leaves'.

Notes

- Yellowwoods are gymnosperms – from the Greek *gymno* (naked) and *sperm* (seed) meaning that the seeds are not enclosed in an ovary. Therefore, they are not flowering plants.
- Gymnosperms are woody plants. Better-known members are pines, cypresses, cycads and ginkgos.
- Locally, yellowwoods are famous for their timber and are commonly grown in gardens – especially the Drooping-leaved yellowwood, which also makes an excellent indigenous Christmas tree.

Cypress Family

Cupressaceae

~150 spp. globally; 4 spp. regionally, all trees

Typical **Mountain cedars** in fynbos. The clumping results from post-fire re-sprouting.

The mature female cones of a **Mountain cedar**.

All cedars, like this **Willowmore cedar**, have leaves that are reduced to tiny clasping scales.

The mature female cones of the **Willowmore cedar** have a more 'warty' appearance than those of the Mountain cedar.

In southern Africa the main representatives of this family are cedars (actual 'cypresses' do not occur in the region). Cedar species are all easy to recognise:

- ✓ leaves reduced to tiny scales, and may be opposite or whorled
- ✓ young trees have a thin conical canopy, only spreading in older trees
- ✓ cones are unisexual and wind pollinated (common to all cedars)
- ✓ female cones are woody, 15–25 mm in diameter, with only a few scales, all of more or less equal size and often clustered in small bunches

The **Mountain cedar** (*Widdringtonia nodiflora*) is the most widespread species in the region. It is an afromontane specialist in fynbos and grassland, and sometimes also occurs on forest edges. It is the only re-sprouter in the family, and is often multi-stemmed. This small tree may attain a maximum of 10 m – but this is not usual.

The two other cedars are the **Clanwilliam cedar** (*W. cedarbergensis*), which is restricted to the Cederberg Mountains and occurs in

A young **Willowmore cedar** growing in a spot where seeds were scattered following a fynbos fire in 1985. Note other individuals in the background.

A rare, large, mature **Clanwilliam cedar**. This specimen has been able to grow because the surrounding boulders offer protection from fire.

greatly diminished numbers because of timber exploitation and frequent fires; and the **Willowmore cedar** (*W. schwarzii*) in the Baviaanskloof Mountains, which has suffered the same fate and is even rarer. The latter can reputedly be very tall (to 40 m) while the former is smaller (<10 m).

SIMILAR SPECIES: The **Wild tamarisk** (*Tamarix usneoides*), a member of the tamarisk family, may be mistaken for a cedar because it has scale-like leaves. It occurs as a gregarious, multi-branched, greyish-green shrub or small tree of 5–6 m, usually fringing brackish rivers in arid areas in the north and west. It is also a stream-bank species in the eastern Karoo and Northern Cape. The tiny cream flowers occur in delicate sprays.

Wild tamarisk leaves are salty to the taste because the species is able to excrete excess salts, which then crystallise on the leaves.

A tall, thin, young **Clanwilliam cedar** growing adjacent to a sandstone boulder. This tree should prosper, given that the rocks not only protect it from fire, but also channel water to its roots.

EvJ

Notes

- Cedars are valued for their timber and have been widely exploited. In Malawi cedars are still being harvested from Mount Mulanje.
- Much effort is being put into re-establishing the Clanwilliam cedar.

Hernandia Family

Hernandiaceae

~35 spp. globally; 1 sp. regionally, a tree

This family has just one representative in southern Africa – the African propeller-tree. These trees are usually of medium size but can be large, and are easily identified by the following combination of characteristics:

- ✓ three or more strong veins from the leaf base
- ✓ leaves are simple, spirally arranged, almost circular in outline (~100 x 100 mm), usually with three apical lobes that are pronounced in leaves on older twigs
- ✓ dark green leaves that are greyish below
- ✓ fruit a hard, woody, two-winged 'nut'
- ✓ plants can exude a white latex if a young leaf is detached

In Namibia **African propeller-trees** (*Gyrocarpus americanus*) occur on dolomite in the north; in the Zambezi and Limpopo valleys they usually grow in hot, dry, low-altitude bushveld.

More tropical than subtropical, the trees are deciduous, usually with a good straight trunk and smooth grey to whitish bark.

WS

These maturing fruits are still plump and green with pale green wings.

BC

On old **African propeller-trees** the leaves tend to have three deep lobes.

BC

Mature seeds have shrivelled fruit and papery wings. Note that the young leaves are clustered apically.

HFG

The leaves on young wood and coppice shoots may be fairly round and unlobed.

Notes

- The common name is derived from the two wings on the fruit, which rotate like slow-moving propeller blades when the fruit falls, allowing the seed to travel some distance from the parent tree.
- The roots and bark are used medicinally.

Lemonwood Family

Monimiaceae ~200 spp. globally; 1 sp. regionally, a tree

This is a southern-hemisphere, mainly tropical and sub-tropical family of shrubs and trees. The trees are characterised by:

- ✓ trunks that are usually not straight, are often multi-stemmed, and have pale bark, flaking to leave faint concentric rings in roundish patches (100–300 mm)
- ✓ leaves that are simple, opposite to sub-opposite (60–140 mm), dark green and glossy above with conspicuous venation, slightly quilted and usually with obvious toothed margins

The **Forest lemonwood** (*Xymalos monospora*) is an afromontane forest-canopy tree found on rocky sites, often in groves. It can also occur in rocky scrub as it is a hardy species that is bird dispersed. This species occurs from just east of Grahamstown, along the Drakensberg and Lebombo ranges, and in the Chimanimani Mountains.

AS

Forest lemonwoods have pale bark that flakes off to reveal diagnostic concentric markings. Note that the freshly exposed surface lacks a covering of lichens and bryophytes.

Older specimens typically have many young and intermediate-aged coppice shoots. ***Inset:*** The under-surface of the leaf is dull and, where marginal teeth occur, the veins run into the 'V' of the tooth.

AS

Forest lemonwood leaves are quite distinctive in shape and size. In this individual, the older leaves (top) have been colonised by surface lichens – a good indication that a leaf is more than a year old.

Notes

- Trees like the Forest lemonwood that shed their bark slowly can be festooned with mosses and lichens.
- Forest lemonwoods are tough, resist fire and disturbance and coppice profusely, which is a useful survival mechanism.

Avocado Family

Lauraceae

~2 000 spp. globally; ~10 spp. regionally, 9 spp. of tree

Black stinkwood leaves showing details of venation, shape, wavy and entire margins and leaf blisters (bulla). *Inset top:* Details of the bulla from below (see arrow). *Inset bottom:* Bulla from above (see arrow).

This subtropical and tropical, almost exclusively woody family (which includes the naturalised Camphor tree) is named for the South American avocado. It has few outstanding characteristics, but a combination of the features listed below will help identify many species:

- ✓ tertiary leaf venation forms a very fine network (the reticulum), which is somewhat diagnostic
- ✓ leaves simple, alternate, with entire margins
- ✓ leaves glossy green above and dull green below
- ✓ crushed leaves slightly aromatic
- ✓ twigs usually green without conspicuous lenticels (tiny wart-like structures on bark)

The most important commercial and medicinal tree in the family is the **Black stinkwood** (*Ocotea bullata*), an afromontane forest canopy species restricted to South Africa. It is easily identified because of the large 'blisters' (bulla) in the axils of the secondary leaf veins.

The **River wild-quince** (*Cryptocarya woodii*) is a small to medium-sized, forest edge and riparian species with broadly elliptic leaves (30–60 mm long) that have a characteristically shaped apex. The first two (basal) side veins (these can be very faint) tend to hug the leaf margin, which is wavy. This tree is found from Grahamstown to the Lebombo Mountains.

The leaves of the **River wild-quince** are glossy, have an elongated drip-tip with a rounded apex, and have wavy margins. *Inset:* Two fine basal veins run some distance along the leaf margin (see arrows) in all wild-quince species; in some species they are more conspicuous.

AS

The leaves of the **Broad-leaved wild-quince** are glossy above. Young leaves may be partly covered in velvety brown hairs.

The **Broad-leaved wild-quince** (*C. latifolia*) has a more restricted South African distribution than that of the River wild-quince – it commonly occurs as a large riparian tree or grows on rocky sites in forests. Young leaves are finely velvety above and green to pale brown below, with a rounded tip and two basal side veins that are clearly visible.

Red-haired wild-quince (*C. wyliei*) is a small tree of scrub forest, usually found on sandy soils and sandstone outcrops. It occurs from about Port St Johns to Durban. There are rust-coloured hairs along the veins, on the leaf under-surface and on the young twigs. The leaves are characteristically bluish below.

INTRODUCED SPECIES: Camphor trees (*Cinnamomum camphora*) have become naturalised, from Port St Johns to Mpumalanga. The leaves are glossy above and paler below.

Camphor leaves have three strong veins from near the base. ***Inset top:*** Details of the vein network (reticulum). ***Inset bottom:*** Hairy pockets in the axils below the leaf appear from above as small bumps.

AS

Under-surface detail of a **Broad-leaved wild-quince** leaf showing the matted hairs, the two marginal veins and the typical rolled margins.

The leaves of the **Red-haired wild-quince** are small and almost round with a marked brown tip extension. They are dull above and bluish below and covered with rusty coloured hairs that also occur on the twigs.

Red-haired wild-quince in fruit. Note the small stiffish leaves with tiny mucros.

Notes

- The bark of stinkwood and the introduced Camphor trees and their relatives is considered to have excellent medicinal properties. This bark is often collected by herbalists, thereby putting the lives of the trees at risk.
- The wood of Black stinkwoods and Camphor trees is aromatic, particularly when being worked.
- Black stinkwood timber is much sought-after for furniture making. The removal of trees for timber is strictly controlled to ensure sustainability.
- The widely known African white-stinkwood (*Celtis africana*) is unrelated and is dealt with on p. 80.

Aloe Family

Asphodelaceae ~400 spp. globally; ~145 spp. regionally, ~25 spp. of tree

JB

The **Eastern tree aloe** is our biggest aloe. This specimen from Kirstenbosch (Cape Town) is old and therefore well branched. Young trees tend to have smoother trunks. ***Inset:*** Leaves showing the attenuating apex.

Aloes are iconic, mostly small to medium-sized trees with the following characteristics:

- ✓ leaves arranged in tight apical bunches
- ✓ leaves simple, fleshy, strap-shaped, and tapering; ~300–600 mm long
- ✓ leaf margin often toothed, but smooth in some species
- ✓ flowers tightly clustered on apical spikes, yellow to bright orange-red, mostly upright, rarely lax
- ✓ mostly single stemmed, usually with old, dried leaves covering at least part of the upper trunk
- ✓ branched species usually have smooth or even succulent trunks and few, if any, old dried leaves (Krantz aloe is the exception)

The biggest aloe of all is the **Eastern tree aloe** (*Aloe barberae*), growing 8–15 m tall, from East London through coastal areas to Nelspruit. It is a commonly planted species, doing well in frost-free areas and growing remarkably quickly. This species, like the Quiver-tree aloe, has succulent, leafless, branched stems.

Quiver-tree aloes (*A. dichotoma*) occur in the arid west from the Northern Cape to north of Windhoek, and tend to be more branched and stocky (~3 m, rarely to 5 m); often with a round, well-formed canopy.

Another branched aloe is the widespread **Krantz aloe** (*A. arborescens*). Seldom reaching 3 m, it occurs from Table Mountain east and north, below the escarpment, as far as Limpopo province and into Zimbabwe.

Arguably the most prominent of all the aloe species is the **Bitter aloe** (*A. ferox*), occurring

This **Quiver-tree aloe** in the botanic gardens at Clanwilliam shows the typically broad trunk relative to height. ***Inset left:*** Quiver-tree aloe inflorescence. ***Inset right:*** The flowers have bright orange stamens.

Quiver-tree aloes have striking, smooth bark.

A large **Krantz aloe** in the northern Drakensberg. It tends to be less divided than other branched tree aloes.

Young **Krantz aloe** inflorescences are typically conical. As the flowers open from the bottom and start to fall, this shape changes.

The old leaves of these **Bitter aloes** have been harvested for the pharmaceutical industry.

through the Eastern Cape into central KwaZulu-Natal. This is 'replaced' by the similar **Mountain aloe** (*A. marlothii*) in Limpopo, Mpumalanga and southern Mozambique, which itself is 'replaced' by the **Noble aloe** (*A. excelsa*) (not illustrated) from the Limpopo River into Zimbabwe.

Two other aloes included here are the **Strand aloe** (*A. thraskii*), occurring in dune forest from about East London to Richards Bay, and the **French aloe** (*A. pluridens*) – an emergent small tree in Addo-type bushveld in the Eastern Cape and north into southern KwaZulu-Natal. Both species have graceful, drooping, pale green leaves with tiny teeth.

CV (main pic)

French aloes have narrow, strongly recurved leaves. *Inset:* Note the many-toothed leaf margin.

GG (main pic)

Mountain aloes in typical bushveld habitat, with old leaves covering the trunk. *Inset:* The filaments are purple with bright orange anthers.

Strand aloes growing on the edge of dune forest. *Inset:* The leaves are strongly recurved and have tiny red teeth along the margins.

GG (inset AS)

Notes

- Aloes flower mainly in winter and spring and they attract many insects and birds.
- Aloes generally transplant easily, and some even grow from truncheons (mostly those species that do not have persistent old leaves on their stems).
- It is probable that late Iron Age people extended the range and habitat of some aloes, particularly the Eastern tree aloe and Krantz aloe, because they planted these species close to their homesteads.
- The Quiver-tree aloe is so-named because Bushmen used the hollow branches to make quivers for their arrows.
- Landscapers increasingly use aloes because they are water-wise and have 'architectural' qualities.

Palm Family

Arecaceae

~2 600 spp. globally; 7 spp. regionally, all trees

Kosi palm in cultivation.

Palms grow in the tropics and subtropics. They are easily recognised by their distinctive growth form – a single trunk and apical rosette of leaves – and by the following:

- ✓ leaves are large and fibrous – either feather-like or fan-shaped
- ✓ trees usually grow together in groves, and/or along drainage lines and in swampy places

The feather-leaved palms are represented by two species:

The fairly common and widespread **Wild date-palm** (*Phoenix reclinata*) extends from north of East London, along the coastal belt and inland into the lowveld, and through the Zambezi valley towards Etosha.

Kosi palms (*Raphia australis*) are restricted to coastal swamps in northern KwaZulu-Natal and southern Mozambique.

The fan-leaved palm species are geographically separated:

The **Southern lala-palm** (*Hyphaene coriacea*) occurs mostly from coastal KwaZulu-Natal to southern Mozambique, whereas the **Northern lala-palm** (*H. petersiana*) occurs mainly along the Angolan and Zambian border.

Borassus palms (*Borassus aethiopum*), which occur in eastern Zimbabwe, have a distinctive bulge about halfway up the trunk.

Pondo palms (*Jubaeopsis caffra*) only occur on the banks of the Mtentu and Msikaba rivers in the northern parts of the Eastern Cape.

A typical clump of **Wild date-palms** with an apical rosette of leaves and bare trunks. *Inset:* **Wild date-palms** starting to flower.

The sap of **Southern lala-palms** is harvested to make a potent brew.

EvJ

Further north, and where the trees are protected from elephant damage, **Northern lala-palms** may be ~4m tall. ***Inset left:*** The fruits are almost spherical. ***Inset right:*** A section through the fruit showing the ivory-coloured centre that is used by local crafts-people. The outer protective layer is very fibrous and extremely tough.

TC

Borassus palms have a diagnostic bulge in the trunk. The specimen on the right has had fronds removed for basketry.

NC (incl. inset)

A grove of **Pondo palms**. ***Inset:*** A pile of Pondo palm fruits. They resemble miniature coconuts.

RELATED SPECIES: One other palm-like plant in the region is **Livingstone's pandanus** (*Pandanus livingstonianus*), or the African screw-pine, which is a close relative to the palms. This small tree is used horticulturally, especially along beach-front areas, as it is extremely hardy. The leaves are long and strap-like, with razor-sharp recurved spines along the margin. The tight bunch of 'stilt-roots' at the trunk base and the large pineapple-like fruits are also diagnostic. Regionally, it occurs in the wild in northern Mozambique and on the Mozambican side of Zimbabwe's eastern highlands.

BP (incl. inset top)

This mature **Livingstone's pandanus** demonstrates the typical shape and branching pattern of the species and the apical rosettes of leaves. ***Inset top:*** The leaf margins have lethal-looking hooks. ***Inset bottom:*** Fruits are pineapple-like.

Notes

- The Kosi palm has arguably the longest leaves in the world (~5 m). The stem or shaft of the leaf is used for building shelters, rafts and for any other purposes where long, strong and light 'poles' are required.
- The leaves of all palm species can be used in basketry, and/or for making fibre for plaiting or twisting into string.
- The kernel of the fruits of the lala-palm is used as 'vegetable ivory' for craft work.
- Palms have been transported over considerable distances by both people and elephants, so some present-day distributions are blurred.
- In northern KwaZulu-Natal the Wild date-palm and the Southern lala-palm are tapped for their sap, which is used to make a local 'beer'.

Strelitzia & Banana Families

Strelitziaceae ~9 spp. globally; ~5 spp. regionally, 3 spp. of tree
Musaceae ~9 spp. globally; 4 spp. regionally, 1 sp. of tree

These trees, with their huge banana-like leaves, are unmistakable. Other features are:

✓ leaves spirally arranged in banana family members, and two-ranked in strelitzias
✓ leaves often wind shredded

The three species of strelitzia are all superficially similar and are generally distinguished by their distribution:

Cape strelitzias (*Strelitzia alba*) occur in a small area just to the south and west of

The flowers of the **Coastal strelitzia** are held high up on the tree in large, boat-like, purplish-brown bracts.

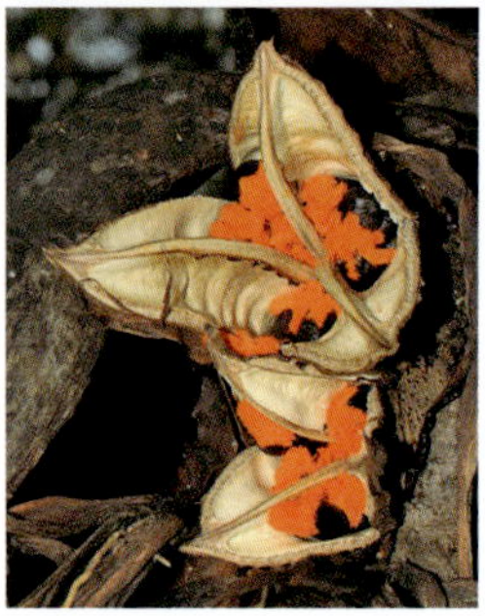

Coastal strelitzias bear extremely hard, woody, three-valved capsules that open to reveal tough black seeds with a bright orange, hairy appendage to attract birds for dispersal.

NC

The large leaves of the **Coastal strelitzia** are distinctly two-ranked – shown here with some old flowers.

Coastal strelitzias occur in clumps that can be quite large, with many stems and plants of different ages. This is because new stems are produced basally. Note the wind-shredded leaves. ***Inset:*** The lower stems are bare and carry conspicuous leaf scars.

HFG

A typical **Cape strelitzia** in forested habitat. Note that, unlike the Coastal strelitzia, neither the Cape nor the Mountain strelitzia generally grows in big clumps.

LT

Mountain strelitzias generally occur among boulders in grassy places.

Port Elizabeth; **Coastal strelitzias** (*S. nicolai*) are found from East London to the Mozambican border; **Mountain strelitzias** (*S. caudata*) grow in the mountainous regions of Mpumalanga, Limpopo and Zimbabwe.

The **Wild banana** (*Ensete ventricosum*) occurs in mountainous areas in Limpopo and eastern Zimbabwe and extends into Mozambique. It is found along streams and often also grows in fringing forest.

Flowering **Wild banana** spikes are quite massive, pendulous and well covered with papery bracts.

The leaves of the **Wild banana** have a distinctive maroon midrib and generally form a loosely rounded canopy. This is a cultivated specimen.

Notes

- The Wild banana flowers when it is ~8 years old, after which the tree dies.
- Strelitzias make an attractive feature in big gardens and are popular with landscapers.
- Once strelitzias are well established in a garden they are extremely difficult to remove. If you plant them, either keep the clump tight or give them plenty of space to spread.

Protea Family

Proteaceae

~2 000 spp. globally; ~1 300 spp. regionally, ~60 spp. of tree

Flower heads of the **Sugar Protea** – after fire the bracts open to release the seeds.

The King protea, which is a shrub, is South Africa's national flower; most people are able to recognise at least some species from this family. The general family characteristics include:

- ✓ leaves that are simple, alternate and/or spirally arranged and tend to be clustered apically
- ✓ leaves usually leathery, thick and fairly rigid
- ✓ mid-vein usually prominent; and side-veins, if visible, are squiggly – ending before the margin
- ✓ leaf margins are mostly entire, or with few apical 'teeth'
- ✓ flowers tightly packed in a spike, a showy head, or an apical cone
- ✓ generally small to medium-sized trees with crooked trunks, or seemingly multi-stemmed from near the base – except the Boekenhouts

Five regional genera in the family have tree-like species. The largest genus is *Protea* with ~30 tree species. They are easily distinguished by the characteristic terminal 'flower heads' that are solitary and comprise many individual flowers, tightly packed on a flattish disc surrounded by tough, overlapping, protective bracts.

Most of the tree-like protea species in the Western Cape depend on fire to re-grow from seed. For these 're-seeders' to reach tree stature there must be a sufficient interval between fires – 30–40 years. Today, however, fires occur more frequently, and tree-like specimens are rare. Two fairly common re-seeders are the **Sugar protea** (*P. repens*) and the **Laurel-leaved protea** (*P. laurifolia*). Sugar proteas are widespread in fynbos and have green foliage, white to yellow to deep pinkish flower heads with a characteristic urn shape and persistent old flower heads. Laurel-leaved

Sugar proteas are particularly attractive and are extensively harvested for the flower trade ***(above)***. Old flowers and buds are both sharply conical ***(left)***.

Laurel-leaved proteas are small spreading trees that occur in dry fynbos. The bluish-green leaves are typically stiff.

Laurel-leaved proteas have 'bearded' flowers, often harvested as cut flowers.

Waboom protea flowers are whitish. The leathery bluish leaves have rounded apices.

A typical small **Waboom protea.** Note the large bluish leaves and crooked stems.

proteas have bluish-green leaves with a tough margin. They are restricted to the more arid western mountain slopes.

'Re-sprouters' in the *Protea* genus include the Waboom protea, found in fynbos, and the Highveld protea, occurring in bushveld and grassland. **Waboom proteas** (*P. nitida*) – the only medium-sized trees in the genus – are widespread. Specimens >4 m with a girth of >300 mm are rare, but historically much bigger trees occurred. **Highveld proteas** (*P. caffra*) usually grow on rocky ridges in scattered groups, and are short trees, rarely attaining 4 m. Both of these 're-sprouters' have spreading canopies with very leathery bluish leaves and bark that is thick and fire resistant.

Most of the pincushions (genus *Leucospermum*) are small bushes – just 15 species are considered to be trees. The **Giant tree-pincushion** (*L. conocarpodendron*), which is endemic to the Cape Peninsula and Kogelberg, is reasonably protected from all but the most severe of fires by its bark. This is thick, corky and quite wrinkled

EvJ (main pic)

Highveld proteas typically grow on rocky ridges. ***Inset:*** Young leaves are reddish. The flower bud on the right is protected by overlapping scales.

Giant tree-pincushions form large hemispherical canopies if they escape being burned.

The inflorescence of the **Highveld protea** opens into a saucer shape. Note its long curved leaves.

A dense tangle of branches and twigs supports the canopy of a **Giant tree-pincushion**.

UNUSUAL SPECIES: The **Cape wild-almond** (*Brabejum stellatifolium*), which is restricted to fynbos, is the only protea species with serrate margins from the leaf base. Old specimens can span an area >10 m in diameter and may be 6–7 m tall.

The huge lax branches grow in a tangled mass; a good example is the well-known Van Riebeeck's Hedge found in Kirstenbosch Gardens, Cape Town.

The leaves are quite different from all other African proteas, being neatly serrate, in whorls (see arrow) of up to 8. They are not clustered apically. The fruiting twig **(*top*)** and flowering twigs **(*above*)** are typical. Note the leaf venation: lateral veins end in marginal teeth **(*left*)**.

The spiky inflorescences of the **Giant tree-pincushion** are typical of the genus. ***Inset:*** The leaves have reddish toothed apices.

– hence the Afrikaans name *Kreupelhout* (which means 'wrinkled wood').

Of the conebushes (genus *Leucadendron*) 19 species are considered to be trees. The **Cape silver-tree** (*L. argenteum*), endemic to the Cape Peninsula, is a small to medium-sized tree of up to 6 m and may be taller in exceptional circumstances (in better watered, fire-protected sites). Cape silver-trees are easily killed by fire and root fungal attack, so the biggest specimens occur in areas that have been fire protected for more than a few decades, and where there's little human traffic.

JB (incl. inset top)

This young **Cape silver-tree** shows the classic silver leaves. ***Inset top:*** A male cone within the apical rosette of leaves. ***Inset bottom:*** Very fine hairs grow on both leaf surfaces. Here they are most clearly visible on the margin.

Fringed pagoda-trees tend to occur in groves, like these photographed in the mountains above False Bay. ***Inset:*** A flowering Fringed pagoda-tree with diagnostic pink-red apical leaves.

Willow boekenhouts characteristically occur in small groves in grassland. *Inset:* The flowers are on long furry spikes.

The **Fringed pagoda-tree** (*Mimetes fimbriifolius*), another Cape Peninsula endemic, is one of two pagoda-tree species. It can be a very sturdy, spreading, and extremely densely canopied small tree up to ~3.5 m high. Where trees are well protected from fire, the canopy forms a hemisphere with leaves from ground level. However, repeated and frequent fires prune the lower branches and surviving trees have a broadly cone-shaped canopy.

The **Willow boekenhout** (*Faurea saligna*) is one of four *Faurea* species that are found in southern Africa. It is usually a slender and graceful, medium-sized tree, <10 m in height, and grows in grassy patches in small, localised groves, often surrounded by bushveld.

Notes

- A few other species of 're-sprouting' proteas can be found, either in grassland or under the open canopy of miombo bushveld. These are always on sandy, nutrient-poor soils.
- The family Proteaceae is the fifth largest tree family in the region.
- Macadamia nut trees, natives of Australia, are also members of the Proteaceae.

Witch-hazel Family

Hamamelidaceae

~85 spp. globally; 3 spp. regionally, 3 spp. of tree

Black witch-hazels have dark leaves. Their whitish bark contrasts against the dimly lit forest understorey. *Inset*: Flower and leaves.

The leaf base of the **Black witch-hazel** is lobed. Note the stellate hairs on the leaf's under-surface. *Inset*: Leaves are opposite and the petioles are somewhat 'clasping' at the base. Brown hairs completely cover the young twig and petiole.

RB

ML

A woody family, poorly represented in the region and vegetatively rather indistinct. But look for:

- ✓ dense stellate hairs on twigs and leaves
- ✓ simple leaves that are distinctly bicoloured with entire margins
- ✓ flowers clustered in dense heads with characteristic ribbon-shaped petals

The most easily identified regional species is the **Black witch-hazel** (*Trichocladus crinitus*), which is generally a slender forest undershrub, 3–4 m high, with pale bark that contrasts with the dark foliage because of the dark brown stellate hairs. The leaves are opposite and have a distinctive shape; they are 25–100 mm long and occasionally grow bigger in deep shade. The tree occurs from about Swellendam to north of Durban.

The most widespread species is the **White witch-hazel** (*T. ellipticus*), which is a scrambler or small tree found in swampy forest areas from Mossel Bay to northern KwaZulu-Natal, on the Mpumalanga Drakensberg, and in the eastern highlands of Zimbabwe. The young twigs are velvety brown and the leaves, which are glossy above, are generally ~70 mm long. The leaf base is not as distinctly lobed as in the Black witch-hazel.

LL (incl. inset)

Twigs of the **White witch-hazel** showing the bicoloured leaves – dark and glossy above and pale below. *Inset*: The leaf base lacks distinct lobes.

The fresh new leaves of the **Splendid witch-hazel** are rusty red and conspicuous. *Inset:* **Splendid witch-hazels** have the most spectacular flowers in the group. The petals are ribbon-like and the broadest in the region.

Splendid witch-hazels (*T. grandiflorus*) are the largest of the regional species and can be medium to large trees that occur in forests, wooded ravines and on forest edges. The leaves are opposite, some 50–100 mm long, and, although conspicuously hairy when young, are more or less hairless and glossy above (and paler below) when mature. This is an uncommon species that is found from Durban northwards to the Soutpansberg.

Notes

- The wood of these species is very hard and tough, and so makes useful walking and fighting sticks.
- Although not widely cultivated, they are attractive species with horticultural potential.

Bottlebrush Family

Melianthaceae

~10 spp. globally; ~18 spp. regionally, 8 spp. of tree

Members of this endemic sub-Saharan family can be recognised by the following features:

- ✓ bottlebrushes are small trees
- ✓ bottlebrush leaves have palmate venation, or at least have three (or more) prominent veins from the base
- ✓ bottlebrush leaf bases sheath the twig
- ✓ in bersamas the leaves are alternate, pinnately compound and have intrapetiolar stipules

The **Glossy bottlebrush** (*Greyia sutherlandii*) is the most widespread bottlebrush, occurring in mountainous areas from north of Grahamstown to Barberton. It is a small crooked tree with spectacular flowers and distinctive leaves.

The **Woolly bottlebrush** (*G. radlkoferi*) is a similar shape but tends to occur in fringing forest, in gullies, and along stream banks in the Lebombo Mountains and northern Drakensberg. What distinguishes it is that the leaf under-surface is yellowish-white because of a dense mat of hairs.

The **Kei bottlebrush** (*G. flanaganii*) is more of a shrub than a small tree. It is found in hills and rocky valleys around Grahamstown. The Kei bottlebrush has woolly leaf under-surfaces like those of the Woolly bottlebrush, but the leaf bases tend to be less lobed.

Of the five bersamas in the region, the **Glossy bersama** (*Bersama lucens*) is the most widespread, occurring as a medium-sized tree in forest areas from Grahamstown to the Lebombo Mountains, at medium to low elevations. The key feature of the species is that the 1–3 pairs of leaflets are highly glossy, dark green above, buff below, with yellowish veins. The leaflet margins are entire, thickened and wavy, and the hairy fruits are 20 mm in diameter and wrinkled.

Forest bersamas (*B. tysoniana*) may attain medium height. They occur mostly in forest and on forest edges, from Grahamstown to the Lebombo Mountains. The twigs are covered with soft reddish hairs and have triangular leaf scars. The leaflets are hairy on both surfaces. The round fruits are brown and covered with woody knobs (~30 mm).

EvJ

LL

Glossy bottlebrush flowering spike ***(left)*** and **Woolly bottlebrush** flowers and young hairy leaves ***(right)***.

EvJ (main pic)

The flowers of the **Kei bottlebrush** are not as clustered as those of the other species.
Inset top: Detail of venation at the leaf base.
Inset bottom: Detail showing how the petiole attachment sheaths the twig.

Notes

- The remaining bersama species can be difficult to identify. A feature of all bersamas is that they occur as widely scattered individuals through the landscape, mostly in forest areas of one kind or another.
- Bottlebrushes make good small-garden trees as they can flower prolifically, producing an abundance of nectar that attracts sunbirds.

Glossy bersama showing the highly glossy leaflets. Note the wavy, entire margins and the terminal leaflet.

JB

Combretum Family

Combretaceae

~600 spp. globally, ~50 spp. regionally, ~45 spp. of tree

Old pods and ageing leaves of the **Red bushwillow**.

TL

This is the eighth largest tree family in the region. Its members occur mostly in subtropical and tropical bushveld, particularly in the eastern parts of southern Africa, with some species in northern Namibia. Family members can be identified by the following characteristics:

- ✓ leaves simple, entire, alternate or opposite, and without stipules
- ✓ fruits mostly conspicuously winged
- ✓ leaves usually with conspicuous and looping lateral veins, and many with (sometimes hairy) pockets on the under-surface

There are ~35 bushwillows in the region (all belonging to the genus *Combretum*), and all but one are small to large trees or lianas with four-winged fruits that can often be found on the plants for many months of the year. On close observation one can see that there are always some wand-like arching branches present on these species.

Most bushwillow flowers are superficially very similar.

TW

A leafless **Red bushwillow** showing straight and upright small branches and wand-like twigs. ***Inset:*** Typical leaf showing the venation and twisted tapering drip-tip; note the opposite young leaves.

One of the most widespread and locally common trees is the **Red bushwillow** (*C. apiculatum*), found from northern KwaZulu-Natal north and west to Namibia (but absent from the central Kalahari). It can be locally common on lighter soils and forms extensive communities. Young leaves have a resinous covering, and the apex is rounded with a fine 'drip-tip' that is often twisted.

The **Large-fruited bushwillow** (*C. zeyheri*) is often mixed in with the Red bushwillow, which has a similar distribution, but the former is rarely locally dominant. It is easily identified as it has the largest fruits in the family (up to 80 × 80 mm) and lacks the drip-tip on the leaf.

Velvet bushwillows (*C. molle*) are restricted to the eastern half of the region and are characterised by largish, velvety, hairy leaves (60–120 mm) and a dark, roughish, blocky bark.

River bushwillows (*C. erythrophyllum*) are generally habitat specialists occurring as a riparian fringing species, often in dense overhanging stands. Their bark is pale brown and tends to have a dimply surface resembling cellulite. They are most common along eastern rivers from Port St Johns north, but also occur along the Orange River.

River bushwillows fruit profusely. Occasional red leaves are typical of some bushwillows. ***Inset:*** The twigs and leaves tend to droop.

Red bushwillow detail showing large upright branches and wand-like terminal branches.

Large-fruited bushwillows have the biggest fruits in the family. The leaves lack a drip-tip.

LL

Velvet bushwillow twig showing fresh and softly hairy leaves and a fruit from the previous year.

EW

Velvet bushwillow: typical fruits.

The bark of the **Leadwood bushwillow** is grey and resembles a reptile's skin.

HFG

Velvet bushwillows have characteristic blocky bark.

The bark of the **River bushwillow** looks rather like cellulite.

GG

The fruits of the **Forest bushwillow** turn reddish as they ripen.

The **Russet bushwillow** (*C. hereroense*) is another readily identifiable species, particularly when in fruit. The fruits are small, ~20 × 20 mm, and a conspicuous dark reddish-brown, becoming two-toned with age. The young leaves can be identified by the velvety brown hairs underneath. They often have a rounded apex with a tiny bristle extension of the midrib, although the bristle falls off in older leaves.

Leadwood bushwillows (*C. imberbe*) can be bushveld giants. Often riparian, they grow on alluvium along drainage lines from northern KwaZulu-Natal and westwards to central Namibia (but are absent from the central Kalahari). This tree is easily identified by its characteristic cracked and fissured pale grey bark – sometimes likened to reptile scales (10–20 × 30–70 mm). Additional identifying characteristics are the short, almost spinescent twigs and the tiny silvery scales on the leaves.

Forest bushwillows (*C. kraussii*) can be large canopy trees. They are conspicuous from afar when their young whitish leaves unfold in spring. Fruits are tinged with red, as are older leaves – typically a few odd red leaves are visible in the canopy. Trees occur mostly in dryish forest at lower altitudes, from north of East London to the Lebombo Mountains.

Wand-like twigs are a diagnostic feature of members of the bushwillow family.

Russet bushwillows are easily recognised, particularly when bearing their distinctively coloured fruit.

One 'bushwillow', the African stink-bushwillow (not pictured), belongs not to *Combretum* but to *Pteleopsis*; its name is misleading.

The 12 species of cluster-leaf all have flat single-winged fruits – a characteristic of the genus *Terminalia*. Another feature is the way the stems divide, producing tightly clustered groups of horizontal branches and leaves that tend to be clustered apically.

Silver cluster-leaves (*T. sericea*) generally occur on light sandy soils from northern KwaZulu-Natal through the centre of the region to Namibia and north (but are absent from the central Kalahari). They are usually found as small trees in groves. They characteristically have silvery leaves, pink-tinged fruits, and dark, almost ropey bark.

In the lowveld **Leadwood bushwillows** can be very large trees (see giraffe). ***Inset top:*** Leadwood bushwillow trunks were once used extensively as the major support poles in the construction of dwellings because they are termite-proof. ***Inset bottom:*** The twigs are characteristically spine-like and tiny grey scales cover the leaves.

Silver cluster-leaves are large trees with blackish bark. They commonly occur in dense groves. ***Inset:*** They usually produce prolific, winged pink fruits. Note the silvery leaves.

Notes

- Bushwillows all have hard and heavy wood that is excellent for braaiing. Some fundis swear that the wood of the Leadwood bushwillow is best for this purpose.
- While many older buildings still have Leadwood bushwillow columns, the trees are now protected and are therefore no longer used for this purpose.
- In the past, Silver cluster-leaf trunks were extensively used to make pestles. The timber can also be used for wood-turning and making small pieces of furniture.

BC

Kalahari cluster-leaves have fairly broad, leathery, hairless leaves.

AJ

The fruits of the **Purple-fruited cluster-leaf** are distinctive and the flowers are white to light yellow.

AJ

The mass of fruits borne by a **Purple-fruited cluster-leaf** can make a striking show.

Like all members of its genus **Lebombo cluster-leaves** have leaves grouped apically on the twigs – as this photograph clearly illustrates.

Lebombo cluster-leaf flowering twig. Note the drip-tips, which act like spouts on the leaves.

Notes

- Because Silver cluster-leaves are not a palatable species they are able to increase in density in areas where the bushveld has been poorly managed. Surprisingly for an encroachment species, the seeds are not only highly parasitised but are also difficult to germinate.
- Many of the cluster-leaves have excellent horticultural potential as they can be hedged and their winged fruits may persist for months.

Purple-fruited cluster-leaves (*T. prunioides*) are readily identified when they bear their purple to bright plum-red fruits. Even when not in fruit trees can be recognised because the leaves are clustered, often on short almost spiny branchlets. The blackish bark and twisted twigs are also characteristic. The species occurs from north of Swaziland and nearly as far west as the Namibian coast. It is absent from the central Kalahari.

Kalahari cluster-leaves (*T. brachystemma*) are also absent from the central Kalahari, despite the name. They usually occur in open bushveld, often around vleis (such as Etosha), through Caprivi and the Zambezi valley, and south into North West province. The leaves tend to be more leathery and greener above than those of Silver cluster-leaves, and their fruits are bright crimson, not so pink-tinged.

Lebombo cluster-leaves (*T. phanerophlebia*) are small to medium-sized trees found from northern KwaZulu-Natal through Swaziland to the Limpopo River. They often grow on rocky sites and along drainage lines. The leaves are typically broader in the last third, with a rounded apex and, often, a downturned tip (like a spout). The lateral veins are indented above, prominent below. Leaves are grey-green to dark green. The bark is fairly smooth, grey to black, and the branchlets shiny and purplish.

Rosette cluster-leaves (*T. stenostachya*) occur in the Zambezi valley and southwards along the western foothills of the eastern highlands in mixed miombo bushveld. They typically have big broad leaves (100–180 mm) with a puckered upper surface and two minute glands at the leaf base.

Pride-of-India Family

Lythraceae

~500 spp. globally; 1 sp. regionally, a tree

This mainly tropical family has one regional species, which is the Bushveld galpinia. It is distinctive because:

- ✓ the midrib ends in a gland (seen as a distinct knob) before the apex
- ✓ the simple leaves are opposite or sub-opposite on squarish twigs
- ✓ occasional red leaves are a feature

Bushveld galpinia (*Galpinia transvaalica*) is a shrub or small tree occurring in bushveld on rocky sites, mainly along the Lebombo Mountains (from north of Durban and just across the Limpopo River into Zimbabwe).

EvJ

In full flower, **Bushveld galpinias** make a spectacular show, although the flowers do not persist for very long.

JB

Note the occasional bright red leaves.

BT

The red-rimmed leaves have a wavy margin.

The spout-like leaf apex and terminal gland are distinguishing features.

Twigs are squarish and ribbed and the leaves are sub-opposite.

EvJ

The fruits are small hard capsules.

Notes

- Galpinias in full flower are an eye-catching sight on bushveld-covered slopes.

Guava Family

Myrtaceae ~5 600 spp. globally; ~25 spp. regionally, ~20 spp. of tree

Mdoni waterberry fruits. Note that the leaves are opposite and then opposite again (decussate).

The Myrtaceae are also known as the Eucalyptus or Gumtree family. Southern African members of this family are easily identifiable by a combination of the following:

- ✓ simple opposite leaves with entire margins
- ✓ secretory cavities often present on the under-surface as minute translucent dots (not always easy to see, even with a ×10 hand lens)
- ✓ flowers with showy white stamens – almost pompom-like
- ✓ fruits often topped by the remains of the calyx lobes

There are ~10 species of waterberry (genus *Syzygium*), mostly medium to large-sized trees, with squarish twigs.

The **Mdoni waterberry** (*S. cordatum*), with its dense spreading crown, is perhaps the most widespread and easily identifiable tree in the family. It occurs from north of East London along the coast in frost-free areas and into Swaziland and Limpopo. It is also found in the eastern Caprivi and through the Zambezi valley. Generally the trees are scattered or grow in small groves in open bushveld, usually in areas where the water table is high. They also occur in riparian bush and in swamp forest (usually in groves). The leaves are elliptic to nearly circular (30–90 × 25–80 mm), with a clasping base and petioles almost absent (<5 mm); they are bluish-green and occur in two opposite ranks. White flowers are borne in spring and early summer, and the characteristic ripe purple fruits in late summer.

The **Bushveld waterberry** (*S. guineense*) is a riparian and vlei-fringing species. It occurs from northern KwaZulu-Natal, north through the Lebombo Mountains to the Limpopo River, as well as along the Cunene and Okavango rivers and in central

Mdoni waterberry leaf showing the general shape, lobed base, very short petiole and squarish twig.

Mdoni waterberry leaves have translucent margins and veins.

Mdoni waterberry flowers are conspicuous against the dense foliage of the canopy from spring to late summer.

Zimbabwe. The bark is whitish and the leaves elliptic (60–140 × 25–75 mm), with conspicuous, often pale pinkish-purple petioles (5–25 mm long). Leaves are yellowish-green to dark green above and much paler below; young leaves can be maroon to reddish-pink.

Forest waterberries (*S. gerrardii*) can be large canopy trees in forests. They are often buttressed.

Bushveld waterberries typically have smooth whitish bark.

Forest waterberry trees have buttressed trunks that can be quite large.

A close-up of young leaves and twigs of a **Bushveld waterberry** – note the tiny glands in the leaf blade and the red twigs.

Bushveld waterberries have narrower leaves and fruits that are more widely scattered than those of the Mdoni waterberry. ***Inset:*** **Bushveld waterberry** leaves. The young leaves of many species in the family have a red or pinkish tinge.

Forest waterberry twigs are squarish and the young leaves reddish. The middle lower leaf shows the characteristic looping veins near the margin.

Notes

- Good water is usually found by drilling in or close to Mdoni waterberry trees.
- The fruits of the Mdoni waterberry are edible, and in some areas rural people make a drink using the fermented fruits.

A **Pondo waterberry** in full flower. Note that the leaves are narrow with a rounded apex, and the twigs are very red. ***Inset top:*** Close up showing the young, squarish red twigs. ***Inset bottom:*** Detail of a leaf showing the translucent venation and conspicuous glands. The translucent margin, marginal vein and secretory cavities (see arrow) are clearly visible.

The twigs are almost four-winged and young leaves are distinctly reddish; mature leaves are elliptic 30–60 × 15–30 mm).

Pondo waterberries (*S. pondoense*) are small neat trees found in forests on rocky and sandy sites in the northern parts of the Eastern Cape (leaves narrowly oblong 40–85 × 30–60 mm).

Cape gums (*Metrosideros angustifolia*) are similar to the waterberries but restricted to fynbos. This common stream-fringing species usually occurs as a small tree; large individuals are rare. They are

Cape gums generally have a few red leaves in their canopy. ***Inset:*** The bark is typically blocky.

Cape gums bear marble-sized pompom flowers that are typical of the family. The fruits are bowl-shaped capsules containing the seeds.

easily identified by the narrowly elliptic hairless leaves (40–90 × 5–12 mm); generally a few old red leaves persist on the tree.

Myrtles (*Eugenia*) are another big genus in the family, with ~12 species in the region. They are mostly shrubs and small trees, although a few are medium sized. Some are difficult to distinguish.

Forest myrtles (*E. natalitia*) are small to medium-sized trees scattered through coastal and afromontane forest from East London to the Lebombo Mountains, with outliers in Zimbabwe's eastern highlands. Smoothish pale brown bark and slightly angular greyish twigs are indicative. The small new leaves confirm the identity of this species: they are broadly elliptic, pinkish (20–60 mm), with gland dots on the under-surface (×10 lens) and entire, slightly rolled-under margins. It is distinguished from the very similar Hairy myrtle by the young shoots, which lack hairs.

Hairy myrtles (*E. woodii*) have characteristic papery bark. They are subcanopy trees, occurring in similar habitat to that of the Forest myrtle, but their range extends further north along the Lebombo Mountains and Soutpansberg and along the coast to Beira. The bark is a little more corky and the twigs tend to be reddish, somewhat flattened and distinctly hairy, becoming grey and hairless with age. The leaves are sometimes three-whorled, broadly elliptic, shiny above and pale whitish-green below.

Dune myrtles (*E. capensis*) are the most easily identifiable of the species. Dune forest specialists, they occur as shrubs and small trees from Port Elizabeth to beyond Beira. The leaves are diagnostic, being tightly opposite, almost circular, with strongly rolled-under margins, and occurring in two ranks.

BP (incl. inset)

Dune myrtle in full flower, showing neat rounded and opposite leaves. ***Inset:*** Leaf arrangement is opposite once and opposite again. Note the leaf thickness, rolled margins and dull under-surface.

HFG

The leaves of the **Forest myrtle** are slightly rolled-under and have entire margins.

ML

Hairy myrtles bear edible red berries. The elliptic, usually opposite leaves can also occur in whorls.

INTRODUCED SPECIES: Guavas (genus *Psidium*) are natives of tropical America and have escaped to become major weeds from Port St Johns northwards, especially in subtropical forest and tropical areas. Characteristic features are the smooth mottled bark, widely elliptic leaves with conspicuous looping veins that are channelled above and raised below, and the winged twigs.

The bark of the **Guava tree** is smooth, mottled and lightly coppery in colour. ***Inset:*** Guavas have leaves that are characteristically quilted, with conspicuous veins that end at the margin.

INTRODUCED SPECIES: Gums belong to the large genus *Eucalyptus*, which is dominant over large parts of Australia: all but one of the ~750 gum trees and their allies are endemic there. More than 10 species are considered to be aggressive invaders of natural areas in South Africa. Common examples include the **Sugar gum** (*E. cladocalyx*), **Karri gum** (*E. diversicolor*), **Flooded gum** (*E. camaldulensis*) and **Spider gum** (*E. lehmannii*).

The identification of gums to species level can be difficult because they are naturally variable and have also been selectively bred, or hybridised, to increase timber production. These 'new' hybrid species use far more water than 'older' species.

Gums are divided into three major groups based on their bark features: very rough, tough, ropey bark along the whole trunk; smoothish bark that does not necessarily extend up the whole length of the trunk ('stocking gums'); or smooth bark that flakes off in pieces of various sizes.

Thereafter, the structure of the inflorescence and the size and shape of the gum nuts (hard, woody, fruiting capsules that usually persist once the seeds have been shed and that range from <10 mm to ~40 mm) are used for specific identification.

The leaves are generally not useful for identification, as they tend to look so similar. They are typically alternate (though on young plants and some coppice shoots they are opposite) and usually strap-shaped, with a tapering tip. When crushed, they often have a eucalypt/menthol smell.

Gums generally have straight, tall, unbranched trunks that frequently coppice, though one species in the fynbos region is small to medium sized with a rounded canopy – the Spider gum.

Flooded gums are magnificent trees with a 'stocking' base, i.e. roughish bark from the base of the tree up to a few metres. They are evergreen and often have pendent foliage. ***Inset:*** Typical gum leaves are alternate, strap-shaped, and have an attenuated apex.

Right: **Flooded gum** 'nuts' or fruit capsules are ~10 mm in size. Characteristic 'teeth' guard the opening of each capsule.

HFG

Spider gums have persistent, woody, tennis ball-sized fruit clusters that make good braai fuel.

Flooded gums have smooth mottled bark and can be huge trees.

Some gums are distinguished by their tough fibrous bark.

Owing to these straight trunks and the fact that they are tough and grow quickly, many gum species have been introduced worldwide and are cultivated for laths, poles and lumber. They are also used as wind breaks and ornamental trees. Although gum wood is said to throw sparks, it is nevertheless used extensively in closed stoves and in indoor fireplaces. In addition, gumtrees produce a good flow of nectar and are sought after by bees. Bee-keepers, therefore, put many hives in gum plantations.

Lavender-tree Family

Heteropyxidaceae

~140 spp. globally; ~3 spp. regionally, all trees

This is a family with few species. They have the following characteristics:

- ✓ leaves simple, entire, alternate and then spirally arranged, pale green and glossy
- ✓ tiny leaf glands produce an aromatic odour when they are crushed
- ✓ leaves usually have a few lateral veins, at least the first two with pockets in the axils on the under-surface (seen as bumps from above)

Lavender-trees (genus *Heteropyxis*) are small to medium-sized. They grow in groves in bushveld and fringing forest, usually on sandstones. They occur from the north of the Eastern Cape through KwaZulu-Natal and west to Mahikeng. They also occur in Zimbabwe and further north and west into Africa. The leaves tend to droop and in autumn can be quite red before they fall.

Natal lavender-trees (*H. natalensis*) are small to medium-sized trees that often grow in groves. They occur from Port St Johns through Mpumalanga and possibly into North West province and Zimbabwe. They grow in high-altitude bushveld, on forest edges and on wetter rocky hill slopes in grassland. The bark is fairly smooth, pale grey to whitish and irregularly flaking.

The **Large-leaved lavender-tree** (*H. dehniae*) occurs mostly in Zimbabwe (as well as further northwards into Malawi and west to the Angolan highlands). It is a small tree found on stony koppies, termitaria, in bush clumps and on forest margins. Although similar to the Natal lavender-tree, the leaves are bigger (up to 140 mm versus 100 mm) and the fresh bark, although smoothish and pale yellowish-brown, may be covered by irregular darker brown flakes. A feature of the leaves of both species is that the first pair of lateral veins, and sometimes one or two of the next two veins, are conspicuous. Pockets are a feature in the axils of the leaf under-surface (appearing as tiny bumps from above).

A third regional species is the Forest lavender-tree (*H. canescens*), which is uncommon and is not pictured here. It is a small to medium-sized tree that grows in ravines and forest edges in Swaziland and north into the Mpumalanga Drakensberg. The leaves tend to be slightly hairy below and have more lateral veins than the former two species. The bark is rough and greyish-brown, with small roundish pock-marks.

Natal lavender-tree leaves have two strong lateral veins in the lower third of the leaf, and pinkish young twigs. The pocket in the leaf axil is visible from above (see arrow). ***Inset:*** The bark is pale and flakes unevenly.

BW

The characteristic dark bark of the **Large-leaved lavender-tree** peels to reveal smooth yellowish bark underneath.

Notes

- Recent DNA studies indicate that this family should be incorporated into the Myrtaceae.

Hard-pear Family

Olinaceae

~8 spp. globally, all endemic to our region; ~7 spp. of tree

Inqudu hard-pear trees may be multi-stemmed. Note the roughish bark. ***Inset left:*** Twig and leaves. ***Inset right:*** A cluster of fruits showing the characteristic circular apical scars.

EvJ

Mountain hard-pears can produce a large crop of many fruits (smaller than those of other species), which weigh down the branches. ***Inset:*** Detail of the leaf attachment showing pink petioles on small 'plinths' on the squarish ribbed twigs.

Olinaceae or *Olinia* spp. are endemic to southern and eastern Africa. Strong family characteristics include:

- ✓ leaves opposite, simple and entire with no stipules
- ✓ young branches squarish
- ✓ crushed leaves (and fresh bark) smell rather like almonds
- ✓ fruit has a circular scar at the end

Two forest-canopy trees occur in the Western Cape: the **Cape hard-pear** (*Olinia capensis*) and the **Inqudu hard-pear** (*O. ventosa*). They are very difficult to tell apart. The leaves of both species are basically elliptic, 30–75 mm long, glossy above and dull below.

The **Mountain hard-pear** (*O. emarginata*) is the most easily identifiable hard-pear tree species. It occurs in afromontane forest from the Eastern Cape north to the Soutpansberg. It has whitish bark and small neat leaves (20–40 mm) that are unmistakable. It can be large at high altitudes, where it is most conspicuous on forest edges.

Notes

- The wood of most hard-pears is useful for making furniture. Many of the Western Cape specimens are multi-stemmed, possibly from coppice growth as a result of felling in the past.

Torchwood Family

Zygophyllaceae

~140 spp. globally; ~70 spp. regionally, 4 spp. of tree

This family (also known as the Caltrop family) is represented by only one tree genus regionally – the torchwoods (although in the arid west there are two genera with quite large shrub species). All members of the family are characterised by having:

- ✓ pinnately compound leaves that are reduced to a single pair of leaflets
- ✓ stout spines that are either simple or forked

The biggest tree in this genus is the **Green-thorn torchwood** (*Balanites maughamii*), which is a bushveld and dry-forest species, occurring in hot low-lying areas from north of Durban to Beira and inland into Limpopo and southern Zimbabwe. These torchwoods can grow to be big trees, characterised by their fluted trunks and rounded canopies. The twigs zigzag conspicuously and have stout, generally forked spines (with one of the forks often longer than the other).

The **Small torchwood** (*B. pedicellaris*) is a small tree that grows in dry bushveld and on alluvial floodplains from northern KwaZulu-Natal through to the Limpopo River valley. The spines tend to be robust and unbranched, and the leaves pale green and velvety.

A similar species, the **Angolan torchwood** (*B. angolensis*), occurs in far northwestern Namibia as a small shrubby tree with yellowish-green leaves.

The fourth species occurs in central and northern Zimbabwe. This is the **Simple-thorned torchwood** (*B. aegyptiaca*), which is a medium-sized tree with bright green leaves and stout unbranched spines.

A young **Green-thorn torchwood** that has not yet developed the fluted trunk that makes this species unique in the bushveld. *Inset:* The fluted trunk of an older specimen.

HFG

Showing the paired leaflets, the stout spines, and the zigzagging twigs of the **Green-thorn torchwood**. *Inset:* The fruit is a fibrous, extremely tough capsule.

The leaves of the **Angolan torchwood** are greyish to yellowish-green. Note the paired leaflets and stout spines.

BW

Bright leaves of the **Simple-thorned torchwood**.

Notes

- The fruits, bark and leaves of the torchwoods can be used as a fish poison, and an extract can even be used to kill land snails.
- The fruits yield good quality oil that is edible; when the fruits are burned, it is their oil content that gives the genus the common name torchwood.
- The wood of the Green-thorn torchwood is used for making kitchen utensils and wooden bowls.

Legume Family

Fabaceae ~19 500 spp. globally; >1 300 spp. regionally, ~180 spp. of tree

The Legume or Fabaceae family (formerly called the Leguminosae) is the largest and most prominent tree family in the region, not only because it has the most species, but also because the species are a major component of bushveld. Indeed, a few of the flat-crowned tree species in the family are African icons. Some species are also important constituents of subtropical and tropical forests. Trees in the family are identified by having one or more of the following characteristics:

- ✓ fruits are pods – though in a few species these have been reduced to single-seeded pods that are not always easily recognised as traditional beans and peas
- ✓ the base of the petiole is always swollen or thickened; this structure is called a pulvinus, and similar swellings also occur in a few non-legume species
- ✓ the family is renowned for the nodules on the roots that house nitrogen-fixing bacteria, which are able to 'fertilise' the soil in the rooting region, enabling nearby grasses to have a higher protein content
- ✓ many of the tree species are winter/dry season deciduous, sometimes being leafless for a short time, or for most of the dry season; the Ana-tree is the only exception to this rule as it is summer deciduous (outside Namibia)

Legumes like this **River thorn** have fruits that are pods. Note that the seeds are alternately arranged.

All legumes have root nodules, best observed on young uprooted plants.

A group of **Umbrella thorns** during a dry winter. Many tree species in the legume family are dry-season deciduous.

JB

Many members of the legume family, like this **Grand umzimbeet**, have compound leaves.

- ✓ many species have compound leaves, but some have simple leaves
- ✓ leaf and/or leaflet margins are always entire
- ✓ stipules (or stipular scars, visible with a ×10 hand lens) are always present in some shape or form.

The family is divided into three subfamilies (although some authors elevate them to full family status). These subfamilies – **Mimosoideae**, **Caesalpinioideae** and **Papilionoideae** – are easily distinguished by their flower structure.

In legumes the base of the petiole is swollen – a structure called the pulvinus (see arrow) – and many species also have one or more glands on the petiole.

Stipules are always present in legumes. The **African weeping-cassia** has fern-like stipules (see arrow).

This **Broad-pod albizia** has a classic pompom or spherical (capitate) inflorescence. Pompoms or spike-shaped inflorescences are characteristic of subfamily Mimosoideae.

This **Pride-of-de-Kaap bauhinia** illustrates the typical flower shape of the Caesalpinioideae subfamily.

EvJ

The pea-shaped flowers of this **Tree wisteria** are typical for members of the Papilionoideae subfamily.

Thorn tree Subfamily

Mimosoideae ~3 000 species globally; ~70 spp. regionally, ~60 spp. of tree

Umbrella thorns – the quintessential African tree.

Umbrella thorns have three kinds of spines: a strongly recurved pair (1), a straight pair (2), and a pair with one straight and one recurved spine (not shown here).

Umbrella thorns carry their diagnostic tightly coiled pods on long slender twigs.

Also known as the Mimosa subfamily, this is the largest legume subfamily regionally. It includes thorn trees (formally the acacias) with ~40 species in the region (and ~1 000 species in Australia) and albizias, with ~15 species regionally. Many of the species in this subfamily are seasonally deciduous bushveld trees and shrubs. They may occur in groves or be widespread and common over extensive areas. The iconic flat-topped trees of the African savanna are members of this family. Most Mimosoideae have the following characteristics:

- ✓ bipinnately compound ('feathery') leaves, many of which have, in addition to the pulvinus, one or more glands on the petiole and/or leaf rachis (midrib)
- ✓ stipules or stipular scars are always present (these may be inconspicuous, and in many African thorns are present as paired spines)
- ✓ the structure of the flowers typifies this subfamily: they are small, regular (radially symmetrical), and arranged in dense inflorescences that are capitate (pompom-like), 10–50 mm in diameter, or spicate (spike-like), 20–50 mm long; in the regional species they are yellow to creamish-white, more rarely pinkish
- ✓ all species generally have pods as fruits, and these may be indehiscent (non-opening) or dehiscent (opening to release the seeds). Those with indehiscent pods rely on being eaten by mammals and having the seeds pass undamaged through the gut to be dispersed

African thorn trees are all spinescent, some having formidable spines. (Australian acacias are spineless.) These spines are mostly paired and are either hooked or straight. There are exceptions to this rule: the **Umbrella thorn** (*Acacia tortilis*) has three kinds of spines: paired hooked, paired straight, and one hooked and one straight. Another exception is the **Three-hook thorn** (*A. senegal*), which has spines grouped in threes: two hooked spines pointing backwards and one straight spine pointing forwards. Thorn trees can be formidably armed – some even have hooked spines scattered on their stems and along the leaf rachis.

Three-hook thorns carry their spines in threes: two hooked backwards and one pointing forwards. This arrangement is diagnostic. ***Inset:*** The fruits are thin and distinctively shaped.

Thorns can be large, occurring in most types of bushveld, along rivers and on plains, but today they are mostly small to medium-sized for many reasons, including exploitation and elephant damage. Their leaves are all twice compound (bipinnately compound) and feathery, their leaflets tiny (generally much smaller than those of albizias), and their pods well developed and quite persistent in most species.

Possibly the most common and certainly the most widespread South African tree is the **Sweet thorn** (*A. karroo*), which occurs in all vegetation types, particularly in karoo. However, it is rare in forest (except in dry coastal forest) and absent from fynbos.

The **Fever thorn** (*A. xanthophloea*) is the most readily identifiable thorn, with its straight spines, pompom-like (capitate) inflorescences and eerily greenish bark, and occurs in hot low-altitude areas in northern KwaZulu-Natal and into Zimbabwe and Mozambique.

Sweet thorn pods are dehiscent, that is, they burst open to release the seeds.

TC

Sweet thorns can be extremely spiny.

Fever thorns typically grow in groves on seasonal floodplains.

Fever thorns are immediately recognisable by their sculptured greenish bark, which is covered in fine powdery dust.

The **Paper-bark thorn** (*A. sieberiana*) is a rather flat-topped tree, with flaking light brown bark (best observed on smaller twigs or branches). It is easiest to find on the grassland-bushveld boundary from KwaZulu-Natal northwards. However, it is also widespread in northern bushveld areas and extends west along the Caprivi into western Namibia.

Camel thorns (*A. erioloba*) are large spreading trees that are a feature of the Kalahari and the arid west. They share the dunes and dry river beds of the Kalahari with the closely related **Grey camel-thorn** (*A. haematoxylon*).

Paper-bark thorns are named for their flaky bark.

The pods of the **Camel thorn** are large, flat, grey and hairy.

Robust spines on zigzagging twigs are characteristic of **Camel thorns**.

Camel thorns can be huge trees in the arid west. ***Inset left:*** Note the ropey bark. ***Inset above:*** Pompom flowers, leaves, spines and reddish zigzagging twigs.

Grey camel-thorn pods are narrow and curved. The leaflets are extremely tiny.

Grey camel-thorns growing in the Aub River valley.

Scented-pod thorns have diagonistic beaded pods: when broken, they give off the sweetish smell that gives this species its common name.

Beaded pods and dense rounded canopies are distinguishing features of the **Scented-pod thorn** (*A. nilotica*). It occurs at low altitudes from KwaZulu-Natal northwards into the tropics and as far west as northwestern Namibia.

River thorns (*A. robusta*) have bright green spring foliage and are most common in riverine bush in the lowveld as far north as the Zambezi. At least two subspecies occur, mainly distinguished by the width of the pod: one has narrow pods (10–20 mm wide that may be conspicuously curved), while the other has broader pods (20–30 mm wide and almost straight).

Horned thorns (*A. grandicornuta*) are easily confused with River thorns, though the pods are much narrower (<10 mm). However, River thorns are riverine specialists, while Horned thorns grow in drier, flatter, hard clay habitats that may be waterlogged in the wet season, and they tend to cluster in groves. Another feature to look for is the zigzagging shape of the twigs.

Horned thorns typically have robust thorns with an obvious boss (causing the thorns to run into each other) and zigzagging twigs.

Straight, fairly woody pods of a **River thorn**. In this species, wide pods tend to be straight, while narrow pods are often curved.

River thorns occur on river banks in low-lying areas. Their bright green spring foliage is eye-catching.

River thorn spines can be robust, but are not on bosses like those of the Horned thorn.

Notes

- In many species the spines can be extremely robust, and many of the trees belong to the 'haak-en-steek' category – tending to snag passers-by.
- Straight spines can be very long (lengths of >300 mm have been recorded) and so plentiful that the trees have a whitish sheen.
- Camel thorns commonly hybridise with Grey camel-thorns. The hybrids look most like Camel thorns, although the pods are much narrower.

Some thorn trees have hooked spines and spicate inflorescences, including the Black monkey thorn, Knob thorn and Delagoa thorn.

Black-monkey thorns (*A. burkei*) and their close allies the **Knob thorns** (*A. nigrescens*) have stout hooked spines (both paired and scattered, some occurring as knobs on the branches). These species occur in northern KwaZulu-Natal – with Knob thorns extending well beyond the region into the tropics, and Black-monkey thorns being restricted mainly to South Africa.

Delagoa thorns (*A. welwitschii*) form dense groves in some northern alluvial flats, such as in the Orpen region of the Kruger National Park, and on the Kruger-Zimbabwe border.

One thorn tree has pompom-like (capitate) inflorescences as well as a combination of paired hooked and paired straight spines and one recurved and one straight spine. This is the **Umbrella thorn** (*A. tortilis*), which is one of the classic flat-topped lowveld trees, often occurring in groves. (See page 56.)

Black-monkey thorns have paired hooked spines at the leaf bases as well as vicious scattered spines on the branches.

The trunk of a **Knob thorn** showing the large, tough, corky, spine-tipped knobs from which this tree gets its common name.

Delagoa thorns are large upright trees with flattish tops and low branches.

Knob thorn pods: note the slight constriction between the seeds.

Two species closely resemble thorn-trees and may be mistaken for them: the Ana tree and the Bushveld sickle-bush (Chinese lantern).

Ana trees (*Faidherbia albida*) are confined to seasonal river banks in the subtropics. They are green in winter and summer deciduous (but evergreen in Namibia). They have straight, paired spines and spicate inflorescences.

Bushveld sickle-bushes (*Dichrostachys cinerea*) often grow in almost impenetrable thickets and are widely distributed from the Eastern Cape north and west into tropical Africa. A number of subspecies can be identified but are not easily distinguished.

Ana trees have broad and slightly twisted pods that are diagnostic.

Bushveld sickle-bushes (Chinese lanterns) have short, sharp branchlets, spectacular flowers and bunches of pods.

Bushveld sickle-bush pods occur in twisted masses.

INTRODUCED SPECIES: Mesquite or *Prosopis* spp., introduced from the southwestern United States and Mexico as fodder plants for cattle, are invasive in western South Africa, southern Namibia and Botswana, while the South American **Stink bean** (*Paraserianthes lophantha*) has become a problem on the south and east coasts.

Some Australian *Acacias* have become aggressive invaders. These *Acacias* do not have spines and most lack bipinnately compound leaves. Their simple 'leaves' are in fact flattened petioles (called phyllodes). The most aggressive species are **Black wattle** (*A. mearnsii*), **Silver wattle** (*A. dealbata*), **Blackwood** (*A. melanoxylon*), **Port Jackson** (*A. saligna*), **Golden wattle** (*A. longifolia*) and **Rooikrans** (*A. cyclops*).

Mesquite trees are multi-stemmed from or near the ground and have a funnel-shaped canopy.

Unlike many other introduced Australian *Acacia* spp., **Black wattles** have bipinnately compound leaves resembling feathers.

Leaves and pods of the **Stink bean**, an aggressive alien along the east coast.

Blackwood pods and a single seed. Seeds of this species have smaller arils than those of Rooikrans.

Rooikrans trees are readily recognised by the bright red waxy ring (known as an aril) around each seed.

Port Jackson flowers. The 'leaves' shown are in fact phyllodes – flattened petioles.

Golden wattle with spicate inflorescences and typical 'leaves' (phyllodes). ***Inset:*** Gall formations are caused by an insect larva introduced as part of a bio-control programme that manages invading wattles by curtailing their seed production. In South Africa such bio-control programmes have been extremely successful.

Worm-cure albizia in bud and in flower. Note the stubby, almost spine-like twigs (see arrow).

Albizias are generally spineless, although one species – **Worm-cure albizia** (*Albizia anthelmintica*) – has short, stout, almost spine-like twigs, similar to those of the Bushveld sickle-bush. In general, albizias tend to have much larger leaflets (20–50 mm) than the majority of thorn trees. (Bitter and Bushveld albizias are exceptions as they have tiny leaflets.) The pompom inflorescences of albizias are much bigger (20–55 mm in diameter) and more open than is typical in the thorns.

The albizias that follow are locally common and/or widespread, and readily identifiable.

Flat-crowned albizias (*A. adianthifolia*) have flat tops and can grow into large trees. They occur mostly in coastal areas north of Port St Johns.

Bitter albizias (*A. amara*) occur through much of Zimbabwe in miombo bushveld, where they are medium-sized trees. They have a dense canopy with pendulous, heavy looking leaves, actually made up of fine leaflets.

JB (inset: AS)

Flat-crowned albizia. ***Inset:*** Flowering twig.

TW

A **Bitter albizia's** leaflets resemble those of many thorn trees.

A single leaf of the **Flat-crowned albizia**. The leaflets tend to be large and roughly rectangular, but terminal pairs are more pointed.

Broad-pod albizias (*A. forbesii*) are found mostly in valleys, along drainage lines. They can be very big trees, with branches that tend to droop. The similar-looking **Bushveld albizia** (*A. harveyi*) is a slender tree with a hook-like tip to the leaflets.

As the name implies, **Many-stemmed albizias** (*A. petersiana*) are multi-stemmed. These medium-sized trees have a funnel-shaped canopy. They grow in the lowveld.

Large-leaved albizias (*A. versicolor*) have the largest leaflets of all (up to 30 × 60 mm), and occur as scattered, medium to large trees, through low-altitude bushveld from north of Durban to the Zambezi, and westwards to north-central Namibia.

Easily identified by its conspicuous papery bark is the **Paperbark albizia** (*A. tanganyicensis*), a medium-sized tree that grows on rocky sites and sometimes in small groves. It occurs from the Waterberg, around the edge of the Zimbabwean central plateau, and in the mountains of Kaokoland.

Broad-pod albizia with flowers and last year's pods.

T.W.

Leaves and a pod of the **Bushveld albizia**. This albizia has leaves that are more characteristic of thorn trees.

Many-stemmed albizias are typically multi-stemmed and have a conical shape.

Large-leaved albizia: detail of leaflets.

A mature **Paperbark albizia** in a bushveld setting. ***Inset:*** Note the thin, papery, bronze bark.

Bauhinia Subfamily

Caesalpinioideae

~1 000 spp. globally; ~50 spp. regionally, ~40 spp. of tree

Inset: EvJ

Young **Bushveld mopane** pods can be quite inconspicuous. When mature, they resemble dry leaves. ***Inset:*** Young leaves appear in shades of autumn. Note the classic butterfly shape.

TC (insets: HFG)

Large false-mopane fruits. ***Inset left:*** **Large false-mopane** leaves have a rather pointed apex. ***Inset right:*** A typical compound leaf of the **Small false-mopane**. Note the slightly rounded apex.

The **Pride-of-de-Kaap bauhinia** has simple lobed leaves.

This is the smallest of the three Legume subfamilies. None of the genera in the region have a large number of species (as is the norm in this subfamily globally). The biggest trees of the miombo bushveld belong to the genus *Brachystegia*, with ~9 species. These msasas cover a large part of Zimbabwe and extend well north into Africa, generally growing on sandy, nutrient-poor soils. Trees in this subfamily usually have the following distinguishing characteristics:

- ✓ alternate, mostly pinnately compound leaves
- ✓ stipules always present (rarely as spines), and sometimes difficult to see, even on young growth; scars can also be inconspicuous
- ✓ flowers tend to be large and showy (10–60 mm in diameter), slightly irregular, with no more than 10 stamens, and are epitomised by bauhinia- and cassia-type flowers
- ✓ pods are fairly robust, generally hard, woody and dehiscent – sometimes bursting explosively and shooting seeds short distances into the surrounding area
- ✓ many species are drought-deciduous
- ✓ fresh spring foliage of miombo bushveld species ranges from reddish-bronze to yellow to bright green

Various species have butterfly-shaped leaves: they may be completely divided (compound), or simple but conspicuously lobed (superficially compound).

The **Bushveld mopane** (*Colophorspermum mopane*) is a butterfly-leaved tree that is widespread in the arid tropical lowlands. It usually occurs in dense, almost monospecific groves that may cover many kilometres. Trees can grow quite large, but are generally small to medium in size and drought-deciduous (shedding their leaves in the dry season to avoid losing too much water via evaporation).

There are two species of false-mopane: the Large and the Small false-mopane. **Large false-mopanes** (*Guibourtia coleosperma*) occur along the northern border of Botswana and into Namibia. They have pointed leaflets (30–100 mm long). **Small false-mopanes** (*G. conjugata*) occur in the east (southern Mozambique and the Hwange area of Zimbabwe). They have rounded leaflets (20–35 mm long).

The remaining butterfly-leaved trees have simple, deeply lobed leaves and are best represented by bauhinias. Of the ~6 species, two are fairly widespread. Most conspicuous is the **Pride-of-de-Kaap bauhinia** (*Bauhinia galpinii*), a scrambling shrub or small tree, often cultivated for its bright red flowers. It occurs on hot rocky slopes or riparian bush from northern KwaZulu-Natal to the

Zambezi. The second widespread bauhinia with a similar growth form is the **Kalahari bauhinia** (*B. petersiana*), which is found in the northeastern Kalahari.

The **Southern camel-foot** (*Piliostigma thonningii*) is named for its deeply divided leaves. This is a small neat tree with a dense rounded canopy and heavy, thick, woody pods (70 × 200 mm) that have edible pulp (hence its alternative common name, which is Monkeybread).

Finally, the **African butterfly-leaf** (*Adenolobus garipensis*) grows on arid, rocky hills from northern South Africa through Namibia to the Angolan border. This small tree has a sparse canopy. Its leaves are sometimes clustered on very short branches, or they may be borne on long, slender, wand-like branches. The leaves are often folded and may resemble the pods.

Kalahari bauhinia: typical flowers. ***Inset:*** This species is distinguished from the Pride-of-de-Kaap bauhinia by its deeply lobed leaves.

The woody pods of the **Southern camel-foot** contain edible pulp.

EvJ

African butterfly-leaf trees have thin roundish pods. When the butterfly-shaped leaves of this tree are folded they resemble the pods. Branches are greenish-brown, with smooth bark.

Notes

- Mopane bushveld covers many flattish low-altitude areas in southern Africa (see map, page 11), which tend to be seasonally waterlogged. On the surface it seems boring country, covered for the most part by a single tree species, but, on closer inspection, other tree species can be found.
- The ~6 bauhinias found regionally are scrambling shrubs or, at best, small trees.

Several *Cassia* and cassia-like species are readily recognised.

Sjambok cassias (*C. abbreviata*) are medium-sized trees of open bushveld and occur from Swaziland to Caprivi, with some records from Kaokoland. In fruit they are instantly identifiable by the long cylindrical pods (up to 900 mm in length and ~25 mm in diameter). The leaves are pinnately compound, soft, thinly textured and green and the canopy is neat and rounded.

The **Eared senna** (*Senna petersiana*) is also easily identifiable. Ranging in size from a shrub to a small tree, it occurs in eastern bushveld habitat, from northern KwaZulu-Natal to Mutare in Zimbabwe. No other tree has such large leafy stipules.

Winter senna (*S. singueana*) is a small deciduous tree found in open bushveld (mostly on termitaria) in central and northern Zimbabwe and in northwestern Namibia. The striking, deep yellow, loose-flowering sprays (up to 200 mm) are found through winter. The narrow, rounded pods (up to 200 mm) are slightly constricted between seeds and are present in spring and summer.

Sjambok cassia gets its name from its long cylindrical pods. ***Inset above:*** The long styles on the flowers are typical of the Bauhinia subfamily. ***Inset right:*** Close-up of an old pod. Note that the leaves are softer than those of other species living in this harsh environment.

BW

Winter sennas are usually in full blossom while the trees are leafless, making them potentially excellent horticultural subjects.

TW

TW

Eared senna stipules are large and leafy. ***Inset:*** The long pods tend to be beaded and can be produced *en masse*, weighing down the twigs and small branches.

The **African greenhair** (*Parkinsonia africana*) ranges in size from a tall spiny shrub to a small tree. It occurs on open arid plains west and north of Kimberley. In an area that is generally treeless, individuals seem to be quite large and prominent. They have ascending branches, and tend to be multi-stemmed, with a funnel-shaped canopy. Hairy twigs – the 'hairs' being persistent leaf midribs – make these trees readily identifiable.

The **African weeping-wattle** (*Peltophorum africanum*) is the last in the cassia group. The name 'wattle' is a misnomer, as the wattles belong to the Mimosoideae subfamily. The leaves are bipinnately compound, and these medium-sized, spineless trees with their dense spreading canopies are, indeed, 'wattle-like'. This is a bushveld species occurring from northern KwaZulu-Natal into eastern Botswana and through Caprivi into northern Namibia. A characteristic feature is the distinctive fern-like stipules that are only present on young branches.

African weeping-wattle flowering spikes are typically terminal and curve upwards, covering the whole canopy.

African weeping-wattle pods turn from green to brown and rustle in the wind. ***Inset:*** Note the diagonistic fern-like stipules – most conspicuous on young twigs.

The **African greenhair** has smooth green bark. These trees are spiny.

The **African greenhair** is so-named as the leaflets fall early, leaving the hair-like leaf midribs clothing the tree.

Notes

- Some years ago almost all African *Cassia* spp. were put into the genus *Senna*, with true *Cassia* spp. being mostly New World species.
- Some species of cassia, mostly introduced to the region for their horticultural importance, are proving to be invasive.
- Where African greenhair trees have been cultivated they can flower prolifically and maintain their leaflets, indicating that they have some potential as good, hardy, spiny, re-sprouting hedge plants.
- African weeping-wattles are widely cultivated ornamentals and are small to medium-sized shade trees.

MH

Mufuti msasas have feathery, hanging, dull green leaves. The pods are produced in a layer above the canopy.

Miombo bushveld extends from north of the Limpopo River through Zimbabwe, Zambia, eastern Angola, much of Malawi, northern Mozambique, and Tanzania. It is dominated by the munondo and by msasas (of which there are ~9 species in the region). Like the boer-beans (see p. 69) these trees have pinnately compound leaves ending in a pair of leaflets. They may be quite large and some produce explosive woody pods in a layer above the canopy. This allows the seeds to be 'shot' some distance from the parent tree without interference.

The most common and widespread species are **Spring msasas** (*Brachystegia spiciformis*). They are found in southern Mozambique and throughout much of Zimbabwe, with a few in the Soutpansberg. The upward-thrusting branches are generally twisted and curved, and this characteristic, together with the pendulous leaves that twist, turn and shimmer in the breeze, helps to characterise this species. In spring the leaves are fantastically colourful.

Mufuti msasas (*B. boehmii*), also known as Prince-of-Wales' feathers, tend to be spreading, sturdy, medium to large trees, often found on poorly drained soils. They occur widely through central and northern Zimbabwe and into northern Botswana. Look for the feathery, pendulous, dull green leaves with overlapping leaflets and large leaf buds. Young leaves are bright red – contrasting with the drab canopy.

The **Mountain msasa** (*B. glaucescens*) is a beautiful spreading tree with a flattish top. It is distinguished by its shape, habitat, and smooth, grey bark that flakes sparsely to reveal fresh yellowish patches. It grows on rocky outcrops, often in small groves, throughout Zimbabwe – wherever suitable environmental conditions occur.

Miombo munondos (*Julbernardia globifera*) occur widely through Zimbabwe and central Mozambique. They have finely hairy leaflets that are a little asymmetric. The leaflet margins have a hairy fringe and the apices are rounded and often slightly notched. The explosive velvety dark brown pods stand proud of the canopy.

TP

BW

Spring msasa trees in full spring glory. ***Inset:*** Note the ribbed groove along the upper edge of the pod.

EW

Mountain msasas have smooth, flaking grey bark with fresh yellowish patches.

HFG

Leaf detail of a **Miombo munondo**.

Miombo munondo pods are typically held well above the canopy.

BW

Boer-beans (*Schotia* spp.) are restricted to southern Africa. The flowers are bright pink to red, borne mostly on old wood, and are thus inside the canopy. The pods are similar in all species, having a tough ring around the edge that often persists on the tree after the seeds are released.

The largest and most widespread species is the **Weeping boer-bean** (*S. brachypetala*), which occurs in bushveld from the northern parts of the Eastern Cape into central Zimbabwe. It is often associated with termitaria and drainage lines. As the name implies, the foliage can be pendulous, and even some big branches tend to hang down.

The **Dwarf boer-bean** (*S. capitata*) is a shrub or small (frequently multi-stemmed) tree. It often grows in thickets on flat, heavily textured soils. The flowers occur in roundish clusters, usually on short branches. It occurs from northern KwaZulu-Natal into southern Mozambique.

The Bush and Karoo boer-beans are medium-sized trees. They have similar distributions, occurring from about Mossel Bay to Port St Johns, but may be separated by their preferred habitat. **Bush boer-beans** (*S. latifolia*) occur on stony slopes, while **Karoo boer-beans** (*S. afra*) are often found along drainage lines. Moreover, the seeds and flowers differ: the seeds of the Karoo boer-bean lack a conspicuous yellow cap and the flowers are showy red, while Bush boer-beans have a distinct yellow cap on the seeds and the flowers are pinkish-white.

JB

An open pod of the **Weeping boer-bean** showing the conspicuous yellow cap to the seeds. ***Inset top:*** Weeping boer-beans are named for their drooping young leaves. ***Inset right:*** Flowers are produced in profusion on old wood.

Dwarf boer-bean flowers are produced in small sprays, often hidden in the foliage.

JB

Dwarf boer-bean leaflets are roundish with a spiny tip.

Inset: CV

Old **Bush boer-bean** pods that have dispersed their yellow-capped seeds. ***Inset:*** Bush boer-bean flowers are pinkish-white.

Young pods of the **Karoo boer-bean**. The hooked tip is characteristic of this species.

Notes

- The word *miombo* is the Swahili name for the msasa.
- Generally miombo country is undulating with poor, sandy soils derived from basement granites.

The following members of the Bauhinia (Caesalpinoideae) subfamily are all remarkable for one reason or another.

The **African burkea** (*Burkea africana*) is medium-sized with a flattened spreading crown, and is found in bushveld from Kimberley to the Zambezi and Cunene rivers. Despite its preference for sandy soils it is absent from the Kalahari. Stubby, densely velvety, rusty red twig tips and bipinnately compound leaves that are crowded apically distinguish this tree. The leaves have an unpaired terminal leaflet (that is, they are imparipinnate), and the leaflets alternate. The flat, thin, pale brown pods hang in conspicuous clusters (~80 × 25 mm).

African tamarinds (*Tamarindus indica*) are medium to large trees. They occur in the Zambezi valley and through the coastal areas of southern Mozambique. They have rounded canopies and drooping branches, but it is the velvety dark brown pods that are the key characteristic – they are indehiscent, sausage-shaped and slightly curved.

The **African pod-mahogany** (*Afzelia quanzensis*) is immediately recognisable by its heavy wooden pods (100–180 × 50–100 mm). The seeds are large, smooth and dark brown with a waxy red cap (25–40 × 10–15 mm). The pinnately compound leaves are highly glossy – darker green above and duller below, and the flowers and pods are held above the canopy. These trees are deciduous, have a wide-spreading flattish canopy, and often occur in small groves on rocky or sandy soils. Their range includes northern KwaZulu-Natal, Mpumalanga and Limpopo, as well as Mozambique, Zimbabwe, northern Botswana and Caprivi in Namibia.

JB

The young twigs of the **African burkea** are covered in characteristic rusty-coloured hairs.

HFG

The inflorescences of **African burkea** form dense pendent spikes.

CV

Typical rounded pods of the **African tamarind**.

LL (inset: J-D)

The flowers and glossy leaflets of an **African pod-mahogany**. ***Inset:*** The seeds are shiny, dark brown with a large waxy cap, or aril.

Zambezi teak (*Baikiaea plurijuga*) occurs in a band from central Zimbabwe westwards to Kaokoland. It is a medium to large tree that grows in deep sand. The crown is dense and spreading and the paripinnate leaves are covered with velvety brown hairs. The leaflets are slightly asymmetric, with a square to lobed base, and the pods are broadest at the apex, with a distinct hook.

The **Eastern Cape umtiza** (*Umtiza listeriana*) is limited to the area inland of East London. It is a multi-branched, spiny, medium-sized, evergreen tree with pinnately compound leaves. It grows among dense bush in ravines, with no similar-looking trees in the vicinity.

The pendent foliage of the three ordeal-trees (*Erythrophleum* spp.) occurring in the region makes them distinctive in the hot dry areas where they grow. They are fairly similar, medium to large, with soft, bipinnately compound, light green leaves.

The **African ordeal-tree** (*E. africanum*) occurs in a belt along the Namibian–Angolan border, from east of Kaokoland almost as far as central Zimbabwe.

The **Maputaland ordeal-tree** (*E. lasianthum*) is a dry-forest species scattered from northern KwaZulu-Natal to north of Maputo.

The third species, namely the **Forest ordeal-tree** (*E. suaveolens*), is found in the lower Zambezi valley, often along rivers, and in tropical forest.

LL

Maputaland ordeal-tree pod and some shiny leaflets.

ML

Forest ordeal-tree pods. This species can be distinguished from the Maputaland ordeal-tree by its larger leaflets.

EvJ (incl inset)

Zambezi teak pods have a recurved point. *Inset:* Flower with a few leaflets.

Eastern Cape umtizas have spiny twigs and pinnately compound leaves. *Inset:* Immature pods, like the leaflets, have tiny spiky appendages.

Notes

- The African tamarind may be a naturalised Asian species, introduced thousands of years ago because its pods can be used to flavour food. Iron-Age people, elephants and other dispersal agents would have spread it further. Conversely, the species may be African and have been introduced into India.
- Zambezi teak is highly sought-after for furniture-making.

Pea & bean Subfamily

Papilionoideae ~13 860 spp. globally; ~1 000 spp. regionally, ~60 spp. of tree

The flowers of the **Sacred coral-tree**. *Inset:* The leaflet under-surface may also have sharp spines.

Coast coral-tree flowers are broad with recurved petals and tend to be an orange-scarlet colour.

Namib coral-tree with new pods **(*above*)** and some from the previous year **(*below*)**. Note the constrictions between seeds.

The second largest subfamily regionally. Most genera have 1–9 species, many of which are lianas, shrubs or small weak trees. All species have the following in common:

- ✓ a distinct sweet-pea shaped flower that may be small (~10 mm in diameter) to quite large (~50 mm in diameter)
- ✓ flowers that are crimson, purple, bright yellow or white, so are mostly conspicuous and rather attractive
- ✓ flowers that, in most species, are tightly arranged on short, showy, spike-like inflorescences
- ✓ pods that vary from almost fleshy (African wild-mango), to large and winged (Kiaat bloodwood), to quite woody (Namib coral-tree), while seeds are either very shiny or brown and dull
- ✓ leaves that are variable, but always alternate

This subfamily includes the coral-trees, which are well known, spectacular and widespread. Iron-Age farmers dispersed them across the landscape and they are still widely cultivated. Some have spines on their bark. All have trifoliolate leaves, spectacular pink to crimson flowers, and pods that are constricted between the seeds. The seeds are orange to red with a blackish patch, except in the case of the Aloe coral-tree (*Erythrina livingstoniana*) (not shown here) of the Zimbabwean lowveld and lower Limpopo River valley, which has white seeds.

The best-known and most widespread coral-tree is the **Sacred coral-tree** (*E. lysistemon*), which attains a medium height, and occurs in a wide range of bushveld habitats from East London, northwards through Mpumalanga, and into the North West province and the eastern highlands of Zimbabwe. It has distinctive, broadly heart-shaped leaflets (sometimes with tiny spines on the midrib below) and bears narrow flowers on tightly packed spikes.

A similar species is the **Coast coral-tree** (*E. caffra*), which is restricted to coastal forest and scrub from Port Elizabeth to Durban, with outliers in the Kosi system (possibly Iron-Age relicts). It is larger than the Sacred coral-tree, its leaves are narrower and lack spines, and its flowers are broader, more open, and orange-scarlet rather than crimson.

Three other coral-trees are fairly similar to one another. They are medium-sized with thick, corky bark. The first, the **Namib coral-tree** (*E. decora*), is restricted to dry, rocky bushveld in northern Namibia.

The second is the distinctive **Broad-leaved coral-tree** (*E. latissima*), which can have very large, thick leaves (up to 600 × 500 mm), and occurs in open bushveld and rocky sites from north of East London to the Lebombo Mountains and into central Zimbabwe.

The third species, the **Red-hot-poker coral-tree** (*E. abyssinica*), occurs in miombo bushveld in central and eastern Zimbabwe and extends eastwards to the highlands. It can be distinguished from the very similar Broad-leaved coral-tree by the knobbly spines on its bark, and by its more upright inflorescences.

Apple-leaves are a group of medium to large trees in this subfamily that are common in bushveld habitat.

The **Bushveld apple-leaf** (*Philenoptera violaceae*) is scattered through low-altitude sites, often on alluvial soils, from northern KwaZulu-Natal northwards and eastwards into northern Botswana and Caprivi. It is recognised by its smooth light brown bark and grey-green leaves, which have paler under-surfaces. It is usually trifoliolate but sometimes pinnate, with five leaflets. The small blue to violet flowers are sweetly fragrant and occur in hanging spikes up to 300 mm long.

A similar species, the **Kalahari apple-leaf** (*P. nelsii*), occurs in hot dry areas, often on Kalahari sands, from eastern Zimbabwe through northern Botswana and into Kaokoland.

BW

Left: **Bushveld apple-leaf** flowers occur in hanging spikes. *Right:* The pods are thin and papery.

Kalahari apple-leaves can make a spectacular show in spring.

AM

A single leaf of the **Broad-leaved coral-tree** showing the arrangement of the leaflets.

HFG

Left: The bark of the **Broad-leaved coral-tree** is characteristically thick and corky. *Right:* There are many stout spines on the branches of the **Red-hot-poker coral-tree**.

HFG

The flowers of the **Red-hot-poker coral-tree** have distinctive frilly petals.

Notes

- Coral-tree seeds are used in jewellery. They are also believed to have magical and medicinal properties and may thus have been carried through the region by prehistoric communities.
- The Forest apple-leaf (*P. sutherlandii*) is a forest-canopy tree that is common in the Ongoye Forest Reserve inland of Richards Bay. It has a strangely discontinuous distribution, occurring in a few other high-altitude forest patches in Swaziland and in Pondoland in the Eastern Cape.

Tree wisteria is characterised by its pendent foliage and by the hanging inflorescences borne in spring and early summer.

JB

Inset: LL

A lone **Kiaat bloodwood** showing the characteristic canopy. Elephants love the bark of this tree, so few big specimens remain in wildlife areas. ***Inset:*** The unique persistent pods have a bristly core and a wavy papery wing (up to 120 mm in diameter).

Left: **Round-leaved bloodwood** pods are flat, round and quite thin. A leaf with five leaflets is also shown – note the shape and venation. ***Right:*** **African wing-pod** flowers.

Notes

- Kiaat bloodwood timber is still harvested in southern Angola and northern Namibia.
- The beautiful Tree wisteria makes an attractive small garden subject and is often cultivated in frost-free areas.

The following bushveld trees, also in the pea and bean subfamily, are worth searching for:

Tree wisterias (*Bolusanthus speciosus*) are small to medium-sized and occur from Lake St Lucia northwards and into Zimbabwe east of the Chimanimani Mountains. They are scattered through low-altitude grassy bushveld, often on clay soils. They have drooping foliage, dark, ropey bark, beautiful blue-to-mauve flowers on loose hanging spikes, and nondescript flat pods (60–110 mm long).

Some bloodwoods are large trees, including the **Kiaat bloodwood** (*Pterocarpus angolensis*), which occurs in mixed bushveld in an arc from northern KwaZulu-Natal through Mozambique, Zimbabwe, northern Botswana, and into northeastern Namibia, where it occurs on Kalahari sands. Having been heavily harvested for timber, the species is now rare.

Round-leaved bloodwoods (*P. rotundifolius*) are widespread and locally common and are found at lower altitudes from northern KwaZulu-Natal, through Mpumalanga, Limpopo and into the North West, as well as throughout most of Zimbabwe. The leaves can be trifoliolate or pinnately compound (3–21 leaflets). Flowers are yellow with crinkled petals and the fruit is a much smaller flattened pod (up to 35 mm long) without a bristle-covered centre. A key distinguishing feature is the characteristic parallel venation of the lateral veins.

African wing-pods (*Xeroderris stuhlmannii*) are large spreading trees in deciduous bushveld from the central Kruger Park northeast to the Indian Ocean and west to Caprivi. The imparipinnate leaves are spirally arranged and crowded on the twig ends, with up to 15 sub-opposite leaflets that appear folded and creased along the midrib. The flowers are small and greenish-white, while the pods are distinctively flattened, with a prominent rim round the edge, and can be held on the tree for a year.

The **African nyala-bean** (*Xanthocercis zambesiaca*) can grow into a huge spreading tree with somewhat drooping branches. It occurs in riparian vegetation, and sometimes on termitaria. It is found in Swaziland, through the lowveld, along the Limpopo River and into the central Zambezi valley.

Close-up of the many-stemmed base of an **African nyala-bean.** ***Inset:*** The fruit is usually a one-seeded bean. Here an aborted second bean pod is shown as a tiny bump.

African wild-mangoes (*Cordyla africana*) are large, deciduous, spreading trees in bushveld, sand forest and riverine situations. They occur from northern KwaZulu-Natal into Mozambique, and north and west along the Zambezi Valley. The fruits are unusual for a legume as they are fleshy (40–80 mm long), with a single shiny black seed in a yellowish-brown pulp.

Showy calpurnias (*Calpurnia aurea*) are shrubs or small trees found in dry forest or fringing riverine bush from about Port Elizabeth to the Soutpansberg and in the Chimanimani Mountains. The leaves are imparipinnate, and the leaflets softly textured, fresh green above and silvery grey below. The canary yellow flowers can occur throughout the year as short pendulous sprays.

The **Grand umzimbeet** (*Millettia grandis*), a medium-sized tree with a flattish canopy, occurs in forest and grassy areas along the coast north of East London to just north of Durban. Young leaves are covered with dark reddish-brown hairs, and leaflets have tiny but conspicuous petioles. The mauve-purple flower spikes are produced as a layer above the canopy, and the hard woody pods are densely covered with velvety brown hairs. When the pods explode (usually under berg wind conditions), they split spirally, distributing seeds 20–30 m away.

Large, quick-growing, easily recognised trees, keurbooms are restricted to the Western Cape coast. They are pioneers on forest edges, or may occur along rivers. The **Pink keurboom** (*Virgilia divaricata*) from Knysna has been extensively cultivated and hybridises with the **Western keurboom** (*V. oroboides*). The two keurbooms are not easy to distinguish, but Pink keurbooms lack the hairy twigs, fully expanded leaves, and rounded or notched leaflet apex typical of the Western species.

African wild-mango flowers and leaflets.

The flowers of a **Showy calpurnia**.The leaves of this species are bicoloured and tend to droop.

Grand umzimbeet showing pods held above the canopy. The pods are covered in tiny, velvety, rust-coloured hairs. *Inset:* The mauve-purple flowering spikes are produced in profusion.

Pink keurbooms have been extensively cultivated for their big deep pink flowers.

Notes

- Like the Grand umzimbeet, some other members of the legume family also produce pods on stalks in a layer above the canopy. These species have explosive pods that disperse seeds a few metres from the parent plant. As a result they grow in groves where the habitat has proven to be suitable.
- Showy calpurnias make attractive small trees in gardens in frost-free areas.

Milkwort Family

Polygalaceae ~1 000 spp. globally; ~200 spp. regionally, ~5 spp. of tree

BW

The sweetpea-like flowers of the **Bushveld violet-tree** may cause this species to be mistaken for one of the Papilionoideae in the legume family. Look for the brush-like appendage hidden in the flower.

Bushveld violet-trees have winged fruits that are diagnostic, although the flowers are more eye-catching.

The leaves of the **Purple-broom polygala** have a sharp tip and are rounder than those of the September-bush polygala.

Notes

- Extracts from the roots and leaves of the Bushveld violet-tree are used medicinally, so the plant is in demand in certain areas.
- Polygalas are used extensively in horticulture. They make attractive small bushes and trees, and do well in pots.

Most species in this family are herbs or shrubs, and even the trees are small. Difficult to characterise vegetatively, they do however all share the following characteristics:

✓ sweetpea-like flowers
✓ a two-chambered ovary

The **Bushveld violet-tree** (*Securidaca longipedunculata*) may attain a height of as much as 6 m. Widespread in the bushveld but never common, it often grows on rocky sites in arid areas. It occurs from northern KwaZulu-Natal through Mozambique and Zimbabwe, and westwards from Limpopo into eastern Botswana, Caprivi and north-central Namibia. It has spirally arranged leaves that are often clustered on dwarf branches, as well as winged fruits and eye-catching, sweetly scented pale purple flower sprays (~10 mm).

Polygalas are generally shrubs – rarely, small trees. They have characteristic sweetpea-like flowers with a brush-like appendage. The **September-bush polygala** (*Polygala virgata*) grows in a variety of habitats, including forest edges, rocky outcrops and sandy coastal areas. It occurs from Cape Town to southern KwaZulu-Natal.

The **Purple-broom polygala** (*P. myrtifolia*) occurs in similar habitat but over a wider range, extending north through Mpumalanga and along the coast to Beira. It has narrower leaves than the September-bush polygala and deeper purple flowers, which are borne in long terminal spikes.

The delicate flowers of the **September-bush polygala**. *Inset:* The flower has a brush-like appendage.

Rose Family

Rosaceae

~3 000 spp. globally; ~120 spp. regionally, ~7 spp. of tree

Trees vary greatly in size and leaf morphology, but individual genera and species are fairly easy to recognise by the following features:

✓ stipules present and often conspicuous
✓ margins are serrate, except for species with needle-like leaves

Perhaps the most readily identifiable small tree in the family is **African ouhout** (*Leucosidea sericea*). Gnarled specimens grow in groves on sloping ground, on rocky sites or on forest edges from Grahamstown to the Soutpansberg, in the Zimbabwean eastern highlands and on Mount Gorongoza in Mozambique.

The **Starry rice-bush** (*Cliffortia nitidula*) is another montane species. It grows in rocky positions, in riverine habitats and on forest edges, from the Western Cape to the Chimanimani Mountains. It is generally small, but may attain a height of as much as 6 m, and is characterised by having tiny leaves, tightly clustered on short branches, as well as conspicuous stipules.

A forest tree, the **African almond** (*Prunus africana*) can attain heights of ~20 m. Its bark is reputed to have medicinal properties. For this reason most individuals show evidence of bark removal. Mature trees have rough, blocky, blackish bark.

AS

A group of small **African ouhout** trees in typical montane habitat. ***Inset:*** Detail of the fruit and the diagnostic deeply indented and pinnately compound leaves.

Starry rice-bush twigs showing the tiny leaves. ***Inset:*** Leaf attachment detail. Note the clasping stipule (see arrow) and the rolled leaf margins.

AS (incl. inset)

African almond leaves have serrated undulating margins, distinctive venation and glossy upper-surfaces.

African almond fruits resemble tiny plums.

Notes

- Rice-bushes belong to the large fynbos genus *Cliffortia*, which includes >100 species. Generally they are small shrubs, but some may attain heights of 2–3 m. Most are easily identified by the clusters of tiny, quite spiky, leaves, but some have bigger, softer, simple leaves. The stipules and clasping leaf bases are distinguishing characteristics.
- Peach trees belong to this family and are naturalised in many highland areas. In spring their pink blossoms often dot the landscape along railway lines and around homesteads.

Buffalo-thorn Family

Rhamnaceae ~900 spp. globally; ~170 spp. regionally, ~10 spp of tree.

Buffalo-thorn jujube fruits and leaves. Note that three veins run from the leaf base, which is unequal, and that the tip is rounded. These leaves are shinier than those of the River jujube. *Inset:* The arrangement of the spines on the twigs is diagnostic – one is recurved and the other straight. The twigs zigzag very slightly.

River jujube in fruit. The leaf is dull and has three strong veins running from the base. *Inset:* Detail of the serrate leaf margin.

Trees in this family have no easily identifiable characteristics, although the different genera are easily distinguished. Nevertheless, the following are some features to look for:

- ✓ like the stinkwood family, the tertiary venation tends to be diagnostic, in that it forms a regular net-like reticulum of minute squares or rectangles
- ✓ leaves are simple, often glossy above, alternate or sub-opposite

Buffalo-thorn jujubes (*Ziziphus mucronata*) are medium to large trees. Widespread but never very common, they occur in many bushveld habitats, sometimes in small groves. These jujubes are absent only from fynbos, desert and the central Kalahari. They are easily identified by their zigzag twigs, paired spines (one pointing forwards and one backwards), and simple alternate leaves, which are strongly three-veined from the base and have serrate margins. The leaves are glossy above and asymmetric (25–70 mm long).

River jujubes (*Z. rivularis*) are shrubs to medium-sized trees that look similar to Buffalo-thorn jujubes but lack the spines. Their leaves have a softer texture, the margins are regularly serrate and the three main veins are conspicuous. They occur in rocky areas and along drainage lines in the Lebombo Mountains of northeastern South Africa.

Brown ivory (*Berchemia discolor*) may reach 16 m. It occurs in bushveld habitat from central to northern Namibia, and east through the Kalahari into Zimbabwe and Mozambique and as far south as Swaziland. The leaves (50–100 mm long) are diagnostic: softly pliable, they have prominent secondary veins looping to the margin in a herringbone pattern, and there are pockets in the axils of the under-surface. Margins are entire or may be widely scalloped between the veins. Petioles are purplish, twisted and grooved on the upper surface, running into the midrib.

Brown ivory leaves are bigger than those of the Red ivory, with the same prominent lateral veins and an entire or widely scalloped margin. Immature fruits are green; ripe fruits are orange.

Red ivory (*B. zeyheri*) has similar leaves to those of Brown ivory, although they are smaller (15–45 mm), bluish-green, with fewer lateral veins (6–10 versus 8–15). The leaf margins are finely scalloped and broadest at the base, not elliptic. These medium-sized trees are found in rocky bushveld from southern KwaZulu-Natal, north and west to Kimberley and into southern Zimbabwe.

Shiny-leaf buckthorns (*Rhamnus prinoides*) are small trees, often lax and scrambling, that typically occur on forest edges from Knysna to the Limpopo River, and in Zimbabwe's eastern highlands. The leaves are dark green, highly glossy, with a deeply grooved midrib, conspicuous looping side veins, and pockets in the axils of the under-surface.

Hard-leaves, as typified by the **Northern hard-leaf** (*Phylica paniculata*), all have small dark to olive-green leaves with woolly white under-surfaces and strongly rolled margins. Generally small and shrubby, they may grow to 4 m. They occur on rocky mountain slopes. The Northern hard-leaf is most widespread, being found from the Western Cape through to the Lebombo Mountains, the Soutpansberg and into the Chimanimani Mountains of Zimbabwe.

TC

Red ivory twig with characteristic neatly shaped, quilted leaves and shallow scalloped margins. ***Inset:*** The tiny fruits are delicious.

The **Northern hard-leaf** has bicoloured leaves with strongly rolled margins. There are matted white hairs on the petioles and stem (***above***). The flowers are tiny and woolly (***left***).

As the name suggests **Shiny-leaf buckthorns** have highly glossy leaves. They are smooth with deeply grooved veins and bumps in some axils. Note the twisted leaf apices (see arrow). ***Inset:*** The under-surface is far duller and the main veins are prominent (see arrow).

Notes

- Buffalo-thorn jujubes are generally small bushveld trees. However, in the coastal forests of northern KwaZulu-Natal they occasionally attain heights of as much as 10 m.
- The wood of Red ivory is dull red. Traditionally, walking sticks or clubs (knobkerries) made from the wood may only be used by Zulu royalty.

Elm Family

Ulmaceae

>60 spp. globally, all woody; 5 spp. regionally, all trees

Species in the elm family are easily distinguished by a combination of the following:

- ✓ all leaves have unequal bases and tend to be asymmetric
- ✓ leaves are alternate
- ✓ twigs zigzag gently
- ✓ flowers are pale, minute and inconspicuous
- ✓ fruits are usually small and are much sought-after by birds

Possibly the most widespread and best-known species is the **African white-stinkwood** (*Celtis africana*). It may attain a height of 20 m and has smoothish pale brown bark. The leaves have a characteristic oval shape with an attenuated apex and prominent venation. These are drought-deciduous trees that grow mostly in forest, but can also be found along drainage lines, in mountainous areas, and in parts of the Karoo where there is sufficient moisture.

The closely related **Rough-leaved white-stinkwood** (*C. gomphophylla*) has thinner leaves with smooth margins. Its range is more restricted than that of the African white-stinkwood. It occurs in coastal forest from Port St Johns to the border of Mozambique, and in Zimbabwe's eastern highlands.

A rare coastal-forest species, the **Red-fruit white-stinkwood** (*C. mildbraedii*) is evergreen. The leaves are pliable, dark green and tend to be pendulous.

African pigeonwood (*Trema orientalis*) leaves resemble those of African white-stinkwoods, but are readily distinguished by their more finely serrated edges. This tree is found in subtropical and tropical forest and also occurs in Namibia along rivers and where spring water supplies sufficient moisture.

Thorny-elms (*Chaetacme aristata*) are mostly coastal forest species found in deep sandy soils or on rocky sites in some bushveld areas. They are identified by their dense canopy of dark green foliage, the fine extension of the mid-vein beyond the apex in young leaves, and occasional spines. Coppice leaves can have very spiky margins and zigzagging twigs. The pale trunk is usually fluted and sometimes has tough spines.

HFG

LL

JB

From left to right: A typical twig of the **African white-stinkwood** showing the leaf arrangement. Note the strong and conspicuous venation and serrate margins. **Rough-leaved white-stinkwood**: on mature twigs leaves exposed to the sun have an entire margin; coppice leaves tend to be serrated. Note the venation, the tapering leaf apex and the slight zigzagging of the twig. The **Red-fruit white-stinkwood** is evergreen and has slightly quilted leaves with the unequal base that typifies all members of this family. **African pigeonwoods** have an unequal leaf base that is sometimes lobed. The leaves of the **Thorny-elm** have a diagonostic fine leaf-tip extension and the margins are entire. Note that the leaf base is only a little unequal.

Notes

- White-stinkwoods, which are unrelated to Black stinkwoods, are named for the unpleasant smell of the wood when it is worked.
- African white-stinkwood is widely cultivated because it is hardy, reasonably drought-tolerant once established, winter/drought-deciduous, and attracts many bird species.
- Red-fruit white-stinkwoods are rare in South Africa but more common further north.
- The introduced Chinese white-stinkwood (*Celtis chinensis*) has become invasive and hybridises with the African white-stinkwood, for which it is often mistaken and, unfortunately, cultivated.

Fig Family

Moraceae ~1 000 spp. globally; ~40 spp. regionally, all trees

Most fig species are easily recognised by their typical fruits. Here, tiny wasps are shown on **Broom-cluster fig** fruits.

BW

Mulberries differ from other members of this family in having tight compound fruits. This is the invasive cultivated species.

A **Large-leaved rock fig** exudes milky latex where a leaf has been removed. The production of latex (1) and the conspicuous stipular scars (2) are typical of this family.

These mostly tropical and subtropical trees are easily recognised by a combination of the following:

- ✓ the unique fig fruit (or in mulberries a tight, juicy, compound fruit)
- ✓ copious milky latex, usually conspicuous
- ✓ distinctive stipules covering the apical buds, which are quickly shed, leaving a clear and characteristic scar encircling the twig
- ✓ simple, alternate and pliable leaves – mostly entire
- ✓ usually smooth pale bark, often with powdery flakes

Generally figs are large trees that occur in forest and bushveld habitats. Conspicuous and spreading, they may be deciduous or evergreen. Fruits are borne either in the axils of the leaves on the twigs, or on specialised dwarf branches.

Some figs have characteristic roots that squeeze between or flow over the rocks like lava. These 'rock-splitter' figs carry their fruits in pairs or small groups on twigs. The following are the most characteristic species:

Namaqua rock figs (*Ficus cordata*) are confined to arid habitats in western South Africa, where they are often the biggest and most conspicuous trees in the landscape.

Hairy rock figs (*F. glumosa*), **Large-leaved rock figs** (*F. abutilifolia*) and **Red-leaved figs** (*F. ingens*) are small to medium-sized trees found mostly in bushveld in the eastern parts of the region (although the last species can grow at altitude on rocky outcrops in grassland).

A large **Namaqua rock fig** in the Cederberg showing the basal root mass covering the rocks. ***Inset:*** Leaves are typically stiff and drooping.

As their name implies, the young leaves of **Red-leaved figs** are bronze to red. They make an outstanding show during spring.

BP

A **Hairy rock fig** with young fruits. The leaves are broad with a heart-shaped base. Both the leaves and twigs are hairy.

Some species of fig are easily identifiable, like the **Broom-cluster fig** (*F. sur*) and the similar **Sycamore fig** (*F. sycomorus*). Both are large, spreading trees and bear their figs on 'brooms' – either on the branches or on the trunk. Sycamore figs grow mostly along rivers in the bushveld. They often grow in groves but may be mixed with other trees. They have roughly textured leaves, unlike the smoother leaves of the Broom-cluster fig, which is a riverine and forest species. It occurs from Cape Town along the coast to beyond the Zambezi. This is one of the few figs with scalloped rather than entire leaf margins.

Stranglers are another important group of figs found in bushveld and in forest, where they are particularly conspicuous. They start off as seedlings on a host tree high above the ground and send fine roots down to the soil. The roots then grow stronger, ultimately suffocating their host. The most common stranglers are the **Forest fig** (*F. craterostoma*), the **Coastal strangler fig** (*F. natalensis*) and the **Lowveld fig** (*F. stuhlmannii*). Because so much forest has been cleared or damaged, these figs are easily seen on forest edges, or growing on the few scattered forest trees that have not been felled.

Finally, a number of other freestanding, non-strangler figs grow in the bushveld,

Left: The brightly coloured ripe fruits of the **Broom-cluster fig** can be spectacular. *Right:* The fruits of the **Sycamore fig** are produced in huge quantities on short stalks on big branches.

Forest fig fruits have elliptic openings, situated apically on small raised portions of the fig.

The leaves of **Coastal strangler figs** are similar to those of the Forest fig, but the fruits are much larger.

EvJ

The leaves of the **Lowveld fig** have conspicous net-veins (see arrow) and small hairy fruits.

Forest strangler figs are a feature of mid-altitude forest. They start life in the canopy and eventually kill their host tree.

CV

Burke's figs can be massive. ***Inset:*** Soft, hairy, purplish-brown ripe figs as well as some unripe green fruits.

sometimes occurring as small, well-shaped trees, but also as very large specimens that are often associated with termitaria – such as **Burke's fig** (*F. burkei*), **Peter's fig** (*F. petersii*) and the **Wonderboom fig** (*F. salicifolia*).

RELATED SPECIES: Also in this family, surprisingly, is the **African mulberry** (*Morus mesozygia*). It is limited to coastal forest north of St Lucia. It is a large tree with characteristic leaves, but the flowers and fruits are inconspicuous.

The venation on the leaves of the **African mulberry** is conspicuous and striking.

Peter's fig showing the long petioles, stiffish leaves and young figs.

JB

The stiff, semi-folded leaves of the **Wonderboom fig** have conspicuous, looping, translucent veins.

JB

The fruits of the **Wonderboom fig** are reddish with yellow blotches.

Notes

- This is the ninth largest family in the region.
- The fleshy fig is a receptacle (a false fruit): it first contains the flowers and later the seeds. Figs are unique among trees in that they bear their flowers internally.
- A strong mutualistic relationship has evolved between each species of fig and a particular wasp pollinator.
- Fig trees are an important food source and can be an excellent place to observe wildlife, since many birds and mammals may be seen feeding in the canopy of a fruiting fig, or on the fallen fruits.

Waxberry Family

Myricaceae

~35 spp. globally; 5 spp. regionally, 3 spp. of tree

The leaves of the **Broad-leaved waxberry** have a typical apical arrangement. ***Inset:*** The upper surface of the leaf has a cobble-like texture.

This family has the following distinctive features:

- ✓ leaves alternate, softly leathery, usually with serrate edges (sometimes seemingly sub-opposite when clustered at twig ends)
- ✓ distinctively dotted, glandular golden hairs on the leaves – particularly on the under-surface
- ✓ leaves aromatic when crushed

The following are waxberries are small to medium-sized trees:

Broad-leaved waxberries (*Morella pilulifera*) are small trees that occur among rocks in mountainous areas and along streams. The elliptic leaves (60–100 mm) tend to be yellowish-green, with lateral veins forming a 'Y' just before the margin. Young leaves are maroonish and the colour can persist on the petiole and midrib. They occur from the central parts of the Eastern Cape into Limpopo and North West, as well as in Zimbabwe's eastern highlands.

Lance-leaved waxberries (*M. serrata*) are also small trees, found mostly in swampy ground. The leaves are narrowly elliptic (80–140 mm) and yellowish when young, maturing to yellowish-green. There are conspicuous golden gland dots on the under-surfaces of the leaves.

Broad-leaved waxberry male plant in flower. Note the twiggy nature of the tree.

Twig of the **Broad-leaved waxberry** with young leaves.

BW (inset: GG)

Lance-leaved waxberries have narrowly elliptic leaves with serrate margins. Note the young male inflorescences. ***Inset:*** Young green fruits. On close inspection the leaves bear a mass of golden gland dots.

Spikethorn Family

Celastraceae ~1 300 spp. globally; ~60 spp. regionally, ~40 spp. of tree

This family of woody plants is the fifth largest in the region and has few easily identifiable characteristics. It includes some of the most difficult species to identify, although experienced tree spotters are able to recognise the 'celastraceous look' – this has to do with the leaf venation, which can be somewhat translucent. Some shared family characteristics include the following:

- ✓ young twigs tend to be greenish and angular
- ✓ leaves are simple, usually alternate and can be in tight clusters (but in some they are sub-opposite)
- ✓ leaves are generally stiffish and leathery
- ✓ stipules are present; usually minute, and are shrivelled and brown even on young shoots
- ✓ flowers are small, white or greenish, rather flat with distinctive nectar-secreting discs around the ovary that can be minute

Spikethorns and the similar false-spikethorns form a group that is fairly easy to recognise, but some species are extremely variable, and fruits are generally required for certain identification. There are ~25 species in the region and only ~7 trees, and all have dwarf, spine-tipped branches. Generally the spines are stout and prolific (30–70 mm long and occasionally much longer).

Pioneer spikethorns (*Gymnosporia buxifolia*) are widespread throughout the region, but absent from the Namib, the Kalahari and northern Zimbabwe. This tree is locally common in many habitats. Its growth form, bark type and leaf size and shape vary. Leaves are generally broader towards the apex, which is usually rounded; they tend to be clustered on short branches, are dull green and mostly shallowly toothed especially in the upper half. The fruit, a three-lobed capsule, is green-yellow at first, grey-brown and wrinkled when ripe.

Another widespread species is the **Red spikethorn** (*G. senegalensis*). A spreading shrub to small tree, it has pale blue-green leaves with a whitish bloom and many regular rounded teeth along the margins. Twigs tend to be wine red, and fruits globose. They are quite common in bushveld in the subtropics (but are absent from the Kalahari).

BW

Red spikethorn leaves are thick and leathery with hard, small-toothed margins.

Members of the spikethorn family, like this **Bushveld saffron**, have tiny, flattish, green flowers.

The spikethorn family has few easily identifiable characteristics, but this **Forest spoonwood** leaf typifies the celastraceous look: slightly opaque squiggly veins and translucent margins.

JE (inset)

Pioneer spikethorn fruits amid dense spikes. ***Inset:*** These trees can be covered in a mass of sweet-smelling whitish flowers. Note the ever-present spines.

White-spotted forest spikethorns (*G. nemorosa*) occur in forest and on forest edges from Knysna to KwaZulu-Natal and Swaziland. Features that distinguish this species are twigs with small pale yellow lenticels, shiny brown spines that are dwarf twigs (and rarely have leaves), and pear-shaped fruiting capsules.

Among the non-spiny family members, the most easily identifiable is the **Drip-tip silky-bark** (*Maytenus acuminata*). This medium-sized tree occurs in forests, on rocky outcrops and along streams from the Cape to Zimbabwe's eastern highlands. Its twigs and petioles tend to be reddish and the leaf apex is generally tapering. Despite the fact that leaf size and shape vary considerably, when the leaves are gently broken and slowly pulled apart, they always remain joined by fine elastic threads.

The only other species in the family that shares this last characteristic is the **Yellow-fruited silk-thread** (*Robsonodendron eucleiformis*). Its leaves are elliptic, thicker and usually have a rounded apex. This is a small slender tree that grows in coastal forest from Cape Town to the Lebombo Mountains of northeastern South Africa.

HFG

The **White-spotted forest spikethorn** is more gracile than other spikethorns and has thinner spines.

New leaves are reddish in the **Drip-tip silky-bark**. Leaf margins are serrated and the upper surface is whitish and waxy.

Yellow-fruited silk-threads have stiff thickish leaves with teeth scattered along the margins.

In both the **Drip-tip silky-bark (*left*)** and the **Yellow-fruited silk-thread (*right*)** diagnostic elastic threads hold the leaf together when it is broken and gently eased apart. However, these are less well-developed in the Yellow-fruited silk-thread.

Notes

- The elastic threads in the leaves of the Drip-tip silky-bark and Yellow-fruited silk-thread are intriguing. It is likely that the cells in the leaves have spiral cell-wall fibres, which unravel when the leaf is gently broken.
- Some spikethorns are locally common and considered scrub encroachment species, that is, they increase in density with poor land management, generally because they are unpalatable.

Another species that is fairly easy to recognise is the **Rock false-candlewood** (*Maytenus oleoides*). This small neat tree is restricted to the Western Cape fynbos region, where it occurs mostly on rocky outcrops. The leaves are elliptic, thick and leathery, sometimes with a bluish bloom, while the petioles and young twigs are pinkish. Old trees have very corky bark.

Three quite similar candlewoods can be difficult to identify:

The **Spiky-fruited candlewood** (*Pterocelastrus tricuspidatus*) may be confused with the Rock false-candlewood, although generally its leaves are bigger (30–80 mm rather than 20–50 mm) with much pinker twigs and petioles, and distinctive three-lobed, horned, bright butter yellow fruits. Their ranges also differ: the Spiky-fruited candlewood tends to be a forest and forest-edge species occurring from Cape Town nearly as far as Durban and in the Lebombo Mountains.

The **White candlewood** (*P. echinatus*) occurs from the northern parts of the Eastern Cape to the Soutpansberg and in the eastern highlands of Zimbabwe. It has reddish twigs and narrow leaves up to 100 mm long. The fruits are similar to those of the Spiky-fruited candlewood but the horns are bigger and softer.

The range of the **Red candlewood** (*P. rostratus*) overlaps with that of the White candlewood. It is found from Cape Town to the Soutpansberg. The twigs tend to be four-angled and pinkish-red, and the leaves much shinier above and duller below, with a wavy margin.

ML

The **White candlewood** has narrow leaves of up to 100 mm in length.

Rock false-candlewoods grow on rocky outcrops in the Western Cape fynbos region. ***Inset left:*** **Rock false-candlewoods** have tiny flowers. Note the translucent rim around the leaves, hidden veins and pinkish twigs and petioles. ***Inset right:*** The bark of a **Rock false-candlewood** can be extremely thick and corky, affording excellent protection from fire.

Spiky-fruited candlewood fruits are bright yellow and often massed on twigs. They have soft spiky protuberances.

Red candlewood flowers and characteristic leaves. The veins are fairly inconspicuous. Note the reddish twigs.

Notes

- Candlewoods are not easy to tell apart, as both leaves and fruits look superficially similar.
- Reputedly, candlewoods are so-named because the branches and roots allegedly contain flammable resin and were therefore used by early colonists as torches.

Typical **Bushveld saffron** with higgledy-piggledy branches. The twigs are sheathed in leaves – they are said to have 'leaf-sleeves'.

The coppice leaves of the **Bushveld saffron** are more strap-shaped with a spikier margin than the leaves on older trees. They are alternately arranged.

The leaves of an older, more established **Bushveld saffron** are grouped in clusters and can have entire margins.

As with the Bushveld saffron, the coppice and juvenile plants of the **Forest saffron** tend to have leaves with rather spiky margins.

Five saffron species occur in the region. The most widespread is the **Bushveld saffron** (*Elaeodendron transvaalense*). These small trees are scattered along drainage lines and on termitaria in bushveld habitat from KwaZulu-Natal north into Zimbabwe and west through northern Botswana to central Namibia. Multi-stemmed, well branched and with rigid arching twigs, they have a higgledy-piggledy look. Two distinct leaf shapes occur: on coppice shoots and young plants leaves are narrowly oblong with spiky margins; on old trees, they occur in small clusters and can have entire margins.

Forest saffrons (*E. croceum*) are small trees often found on the edges of afromontane forests from Knysna to Zimbabwe's eastern highlands. This species has longish petioles (up to 10 mm) and opposite or sub-opposite leaves (50–115 mm long) with sharply toothed margins. The fruits are yellowish and wrinkly when ripe.

HFG

Forest spoonwoods (*Cassine peragua*) are medium-sized forest trees with characteristic smoothish orange-brown bark. They occur from the Western Cape to the Lebombo Mountains in northeastern South Africa. The leaves measure 30–70 mm, and are opposite to sub-opposite with prominent ribbed veins on both surfaces. The apex tends to be rounded and is occasionally notched. The fruit is roundish, dark purple and fleshy (~5 mm).

Ladle spoonwoods (*C. schinoides*) are confined to forested areas in the Western Cape. They have much narrower leaves and larger fruits (7–10 mm) than those of Forest spoonwoods.

Bald kooboo-berries (*Mystroxylon aethiopicum*) are widespread from Knysna north to the Lebombo Mountains, extending east to the coast and west to Kimberley. The species also occurs over much of Zimbabwe and in western Caprivi. It is a small to medium-sized tree that grows in forest habitat, riverine areas and even the bushveld (usually on termitaria). The leaves are spirally arranged, elliptic (20–100 mm long), with finely toothed margins, a rounded apex that may be shallowly notched, and a broad tapering base. Dark green above, they are paler and often velvety below, with yellowish veins. The fruits are bright red and fleshy, 10–20 mm.

Forest spoonwoods bear spectacular masses of small, sweet-smelling white flowers. ***Inset:*** Detail of the leaf tip, which tends to be rounded and is occasionally notched.

The ripe fruits of a **Ladle spoonwood** are purplish-black and the leaves fairly narrow.

Ripe (black), ripening (red) and unripe (green) fruits of the **Forest spoonwood**. Note that the leaves have been well chewed by insects.

Forest spoonwoods are easily recognised by their smoothish, slightly fluted, orange-brown trunks.

Ripe and green fruits of the **Bald kooboo-berry**. The roundish leaves have even serrations.

Notes

- Saffrons all have fairly stiff leathery leaves that have a generically similar look: matt to glossy above and dull below, with a similar reticulum of tiny veins. If you gently peel away the dead outer layer of bark using your thumbnail there is usually an orange underbark layer.
- Remember that some species in this family are difficult to distinguish, saffrons being good examples.

Wild-alder Family

Cunoniaceae

~350 spp. globally; 2 spp. regionally, both trees

Wild-alder species are generally big trees that commonly coppice and are found in riverine or forest habitats. They have the following features:

- ✓ leaves opposite and either trifoliolate or pinnately compound; quite large, generally >150 mm long
- ✓ leaflets with serrate margins
- ✓ big stipules that leave large obvious scars when they fall
- ✓ upright growth habit, but may sometimes lean over stream banks

The most common and widespread species is the **African red-alder** (*Cunonia capensis*), which has conspicuous 'butter spoon' stipules and compound (imparipinnate) leaves. In the Western Cape this is both a riverine and wet-forest species. It also occurs in forest further north, as far as the border of Mozambique.

Cape white-alders (*Platylophus trifoliatus*) are restricted to rivers in the Western Cape and afromontane forest from Betty's Bay to Mossel Bay. It has opposite, trifoliolate leaves and is essentially a riverine specialist.

The conspicuous, paired, candle-like inflorescences of the **African red-alder** are diagonistic.

Left: Close-up of the diagnostic stipules (often referred to as 'butter spoons') of an **African red-alder.** *Right:* A young leaf starting to unfold from the protective stipules and the remains of the 'butter' – the whitish waxy substance that surrounds the bud when the stipules are closed.

Cape white-alders are typically large trees found in riparian vegetation. ***Inset:*** Fruiting twig illustrating the opposite compound leaves and serrated margins that are characteristic of members of this family.

Notes

- If the 'butter spoons' are carefully prised open they reveal a sticky white paste – this is the 'butter'.
- Many tree species in the region have large stipules (including members of the wild-alder, fig and coffee families) that function to protect the apical or axillary buds from being eaten when young.

Onionwood Family

Rhizophoraceae

~120 spp. globally; ~10 spp. regionally, all trees

This family includes the Red and Black mangroves (dealt with separately on pp. 16–17). Onionwoods are medium-sized forest trees, and are recognised by the following features:

- ✓ leaves simple, opposite or three-whorled
- ✓ leaf edges not entire, especially towards the apex (although some are entire in the Large-leaved onionwood)

The **Large-leaved onionwood** (*Cassipourea gummiflua*) can attain medium height. The leaves of this evergreen tree are mostly three-whorled, broadly elliptic, have margins that can be finely toothed towards the apex, and are glossy above and dull below. This onionwood occurs from Port St Johns to northern KwaZulu-Natal and in the Chimanimani Mountains.

African onionwoods (*C. malosana*) are small to medium-sized trees. The branches grow in nearly horizontal tiers, giving the tree a symmetrical appearance. The species occurs from north of East London to the Lebombo Mountains, on the eastern border of Zimbabwe and into Mozambique.

Large-leaved onionwoods have glossy opposite leaves. They are generally arranged in whorls of three.

The old flowers of a **Large-leaved onionwood** are held in tight bunches in the leaf axils.

African onionwoods have more or less horizontal branches, as can be seen in this young forest tree.

African onionwood leaves, particularly the coppice leaves, may have quite spiky margins.

Typical opposite leaves and smooth dark twigs of the **African onionwood**.

Euphorbia Family

Euphorbiaceae ~7 500 spp. globally; ~400 spp. regionally, ~100 spp. of tree

Naboom euphorbias are large bushveld trees with a dense canopy.

A heterogeneous family, vegetatively and florally. The vast majority of species are recognisable by combinations of some of the following:

- ✓ simple, alternate leaves
- ✓ milky or watery latex
- ✓ a pair of glands where the petiole joins the leaf blade
- ✓ stipules (and hence stipular scars) present
- ✓ fruits that are three-lobed/chambered

One group in the family is readily identifiable. This is the genus *Euphorbia*, which includes ~18 species that are largely leafless, succulent-stemmed, small to medium-sized trees, most of which bear spines on small shields. Euphorbias often occur in groves and all have extremely toxic and copious milky latex as well as leaves that last just a few weeks.

The most massive is the **Naboom euphorbia** (*E. ingens*), which can be as much as 10 m tall and has a dense rounded canopy.

Other medium to large bushveld species that have single trunks and rounded canopies are the **Lebombo euphorbia** (*E. confinalis*) and the more widely distributed **Deadliest euphorbia** (*E. cooperi*). In the former species the stem segments are long and not conspicuously separated; in the latter they are broader at the base and well segmented.

The **Lebombo euphorbia** tends to grow in small groves, often on steep rocky sites and cliffs. ***Inset:*** The stems have prominant paired spines borne on small shields.

The stem segments of the **Deadliest euphorbia** are deltoid in shape. ***Inset:*** The fruits are typical of the genus. Note how the spine shields fuse with one another.

Three euphorbias in the region can attain heights of 6–8 m (and may be taller in steep areas). They generally occur in dense groves, usually on steep, hot, north- and west-facing rocky slopes and cliffs. They are the Valley-bush, Honey and River euphorbias.

The **Valley-bush euphorbia** (*E. grandidens*) occurs from Grahamstown to southern Mpumalanga, usually in valley bushveld.

The **Honey euphorbia** (*E. tetragona*) has a similar distribution and co-occurs with the Valley-bush euphorbia but does not extend much further north than Durban.

Co-occurring with the previous two species, the **River euphorbia** (*E. triangularis*) is found from Grahamstown to Swaziland and into the southern parts of Mozambique.

The **Rubber-hedge euphorbia** (*E. tirucalli*) is quite different from all the previous species because it has round, not angular, stems that have no spines. There is some evidence that this more widespread bushveld species, most common in the Thukela River Basin, was introduced from India in the Iron Age both as a hedge plant and for its reputed magical properties. This species cannot be confused with other euphorbias. There is a climber that looks similar, but it is never a tree, and the stems are wand-like, not stiff and erect.

River euphorbias get the scientific name *triangularis* from their three-angled twigs. The twigs are segmented, and can photo-synthesise.

BW

A very old and large **Rubber-hedge euphorbia.** ***Inset:*** The stems are round, not angular, and can bear tiny ephemeral leaves in the wet season.

Valley-bush euphorbias have flattened photosynthetic stems **(*left*)**. On the main branches and trunk the remnants of the spine-bearing shields are often conspicuous **(*right*)**.

This pair of **Honey euphorbias** was planted many years ago to mark the birth of twins at an old homestead that has long since disappeared. ***Inset:*** The photosynthetic stems are squarish – hence the scientific name *tetragona*, which means 'four-sided'.

Notes

- With ~100 species in the region, Euphorbiaceae is the second biggest tree family.
- Some local people plant two euphorbias next to their homestead when twins are born.
- Honey made from some species of Euphorbiaceae can be toxic to humans.
- A number of herbivores, particularly black rhinos, regularly browse on succulent euphorbias, as they are immune to the toxic substances in these plants.
- In humans, the latex can cause severe burning in the eyes and mouth and blindness may result.
- The planting of Rubber-hedge euphorbia is believed by some to ward off evil spirits and keep lightning away from the homestead.

EvJ

A grove of huge **Bushveld manketti-trees** that have been left standing in a cultivated field.

Lebombo ironwoods have leathery opposite leaves. They are white and velvety below and the petiole is peltate – attached well within the blade (see arrow).

Bushveld tamboti has characteristic dark bark with a fairly regular, rectangular, blocky structure.

TC

Bushveld mahobohobos have delicious round fruits and large leaves that are spirally arranged.

Notes

- Bushveld manketti-trees produce fruits from which 'nuts' are collected. They are a valuable source of food – and so the trees are not cleared in agricultural land.
- Bushveld tamboti fruits sometimes contain larvae that can cause the fruits to 'jump', especially when they fall in hot sunny places.
- Bushveld mahobohobo groves indicate prime tobacco-growing land, so large areas have been cleared for cultivation.

The following trees belonging to the Euphorbiaceae usually have readily visible milky latex:

The **Bushveld manketti-tree** (*Schinziophyton rautanenii*) occurs through the bushveld of the Caprivi and into Zimbabwe and the northern Kalahari. It has digitally compound leaves (60–170 mm long) and is a large, neat, spreading, deciduous tree that may attain 6–15 m in height. The nuts are edible and sought-after.

Lebombo ironwoods (*Androstachys johnsonii*) are evergreen trees, can be large, and are found in small tight groves on rocky sites from northern KwaZulu-Natal into southern Zimbabwe. The opposite, neat, heart-shaped leaves are distinctly bicoloured (25–60 mm long).

The **Bushveld tamboti** (*Spirostachys africana*) is a medium-sized, deciduous bushveld tree, often found in low-lying areas or on hillsides, usually in loose groves. It occurs in northern and central Namibia, southern Zimbabwe and Mozambique, and eastern Botswana. In South Africa it occurs in the northern parts of the Eastern Cape, through KwaZulu-Natal, and throughout the middleveld and lowveld of Mpumalanga, Limpopo, Gauteng and North West. The alternate leaves have a finely serrate margin (20–75 mm long). Key features are the blocky or rectangular, almost black bark, and the occasional red leaves scattered through the canopy.

Several species of **Bushveld mahobohobo** (*Uapaca* spp.) occur in the miombo. Mostly trees, they grow in scattered groves on light soils. The leaves are large (80–180 mm long), spirally arranged and clustered on brittle thickish twigs. They have prominent side-veins and a rounded apex. The round fruits measure up to 25 mm and are sweet and delicious.

Bushveld duiker-berries (*Sclerocroton integerrimus*) are small deciduous trees, usually found in thicket along the coast and on forest edges, from about Port St Johns to southern Mozambique. The leaves are thin, slightly serrate (25–80 mm), with a bluish under-surface. Twigs tend to be a little arching or pendulous.

River macarangas (*Macaranga capensis*) are large to medium-sized, straight-stemmed, forest-edge trees occurring along the coast from Port St Johns to Mozambique and on the Chimanimani Mountains. Leaves on young trees can be very large with serrate margins. Generally, however, the heart-shaped leaves are smaller (100–150 mm) with three prominent veins from the base. The leaf stalk is attached from below (a distinguishing characteristic of the species).

CV

Bushveld duiker-berries have ribbed fruits with a persistent style.

TA

Young hairy leaves of a **River macaranga.** Note the long petioles.

The Euphorbiaceae that follow generally lack milky or watery latex, or their latex is difficult to find.

Crotons usually have a pair of stalked glands at the base of the leaf (a ×10 hand lens may be useful here) and can be locally common. Some species have distinctly bicoloured leaves.

The **Lavender croton** (*Croton gratissimus*) is a small to medium-sized bushveld tree of the tropics and subtropics and is usually found on rocky sites. Its leaves are almost silvery below and have ginger scales.

The **Fever-berry croton** (*C. megalobotrys*) is a shrubby medium-sized tree occurring on alluvial flats in the Limpopo and Zambezi valleys. It has heart-shaped River macaranga-like leaves that are silvery-green and hairy, particularly when young.

The **Forest croton** (*C. sylvaticus*) can be confused with the River macaranga as its leaves, distribution and habitat are similar. However, the leaves of the Forest croton are smaller and the stalked glands quite visible.

Warty-fruit lightning-bushes (*Clutia pulchella*) are small trees that are widespread at forest edges, in low scrubby forest and in ravines. The leaves are bluish below with a smooth margin. Some bright orange leaves are always scattered through the sparse canopy.

Lavender crotons have unusual leaves. They are bluish-green above and silvery below and may be arched. *Inset:* Detail of the leaf under-surface showing a pair of basal glands and the ginger scales.

Fever-berry crotons have serrate heart-shaped leaves with scattered hairs. Five veins run out from the leaf base. Close inspection would also reveal a pair of tiny glands.

The **Warty-fruit lightning-bush** has occasional orange-red leaves. The backs of the leaves are slightly bluish.

JB

Forest croton foliage and ripe fruits. *Inset top:* Enlarged section of the leaf surface showing stellate hairs. *Inset bottom:* Detail of the leaf base showing the paired, stalked glands, stellate hairs and many strong veins.

JB

The **Stem-fruit ironplum** has glossy leathery leaves with toughish spiky margins.

Forest ironplum leaves. Note the shallowly scalloped margins. Close inspection reveals that both leaves and twigs are slightly hairy.

AS

The looping secondary veins end at the margin, and the upper-surface is quilted in both young (*left*) and old (*right*) **Mitzeeri sweetberry** leaves.

Notes

- *Vaalbos* ('grey bush' in Afrikaans) is the name given to the bushveld around Mahikeng. Trees that grow here tend to have silvery-grey leaves. Crotons are common and widespread here.
- The young bronze leaves of Mitzeeri sweetberries are distinctive even from a distance.

Ironplums are small to large trees that occur in coastal and afromontane forest from Port St Johns northwards. Their leaves are asymmetric.

Stem-fruit ironplums (*Drypetes natalensis*) are small subcanopy trees with glossy dark green leaves that have spiky margins.

Forest ironplums (*D. gerrardii*) are forest-canopy trees with branches that grow at right angles, a fluted trunk and a buttressed base.

Sweetberries may be small to large. Their leaves have prominent lateral veins that end at the margin.

Mitzeeri sweetberries (*Bridelia micrantha*) prefer riverine situations from Port St Johns through coastal and montane areas to the Chimanimani Mountains. Young leaves can be conspicuously bronze.

The **Velvet-leaved sweetberry** (*B. mollis*) is also a stream-bank species, but occurs in subtropical to tropical bushveld. As the name implies, its leaves are covered with a golden fuzz.

Bushveld tasselberries (*Antidesma venosum*) are small spreading trees, usually found in low-altitude riverine situations from north of East London to Mozambique, and through Zimbabwe to northern Botswana and Namibia. They have short flower and fruit spikes (50–100 mm long) that are pendulous. The fruits are tiny, round and often multicoloured.

BW

Velvet-leaved sweetberries have rounded leaves that can be quite hairy.

Bottom left: **Bushveld tasselberries** are identified by their multicoloured, pendulous fruiting spikes. ***Bottom right:*** Note the slightly zigzagging stem, the glossy leaf upper-surface and the unequal, weakly lobed leaf bases.

AS

AS

Wild-plane Family

Ochnaceae

~600 spp. globally; >20 spp. regionally, ~17 spp. of tree

JB

Cold-bark ochnas are readily identified by their smooth and mottled bark, which is noticeably cool to the touch. *Inset:* The leaves have finely serrate margins and the venation has a faint herringbone pattern. The flowers are comparatively dull.

Fruiting **Showy ochnas** make a splendid display. *Inset:* Older leaves turn reddish before falling. Note the venation, margins and diagnostic, slightly curved midrib.

EvJ

BW

Left: **Red-ironwood ochna** – old flowers and immature fruits. *Right:* The **Peeling-bark ochna** gets its name from the way the bark is shed, leaving fresh pale bark exposed.

In the region, all but one of the woody species in this family belong to the genus *Ochna*. They share most of the following characteristics:

- ✓ leaves are simple, alternate, all with more or less finely toothed margins
- ✓ leaves have many closely spaced secondary veins, not always clearly visible
- ✓ stipules are narrow, almost in the leaf axil
- ✓ apical and axillary buds tend to be elongated and covered by overlapping, scale-like brown leaves (somewhat resembling miniature pine cones)
- ✓ all species are shrubs to medium-sized trees
- ✓ all species have showy yellow, rarely cream, flowers

Cold-bark ochnas (*O. arborea*) have conspicuous, smooth, mottled trunks that are cool to the touch. They are forest subcanopy trees, but do also occur in scrub and riverine areas from Knysna to the Lebombo Mountains and in the eastern highlands of Zimbabwe.

The **Showy ochna** (*O. natalitia*) is perhaps the most widespread *Ochna*, and occurs from Knysna northwards as far as Beira and inland to Kimberley. It is found in rocky and damp areas in the bushveld. This many-stemmed tree is usually small and has smoothish brown bark. The twigs have many lenticels, often with galls, and resemble small, protea-like red buds. Young leaves are coppery, and the many closely spaced lateral veins can be obscure. Leaves vary from narrow to broad and from small to quite large (20–120 mm).

Red-ironwood ochnas (*O. holstii*) are also quite widespread, and occur in forests and ravines from East London northwards. They also grow in marginal and upland grassland areas in an arch from KwaZulu-Natal to Kimberley and in the rocky mountainous parts of Zimbabwe. The bark is brown and the branches tend to be held horizontally with leaves in the same plane. The leaves are broadly elliptic and their size varies according to the habitat: they are large in forest specimens, smaller in the bushveld. The lateral veins are conspicuous. Young twigs can be whitish.

The **Peeling-bark ochna** (*O. pulchra*) is a bushveld species that prefers sandy soils and often grows in groves. It is found from Limpopo and North West province, northwards into southern and eastern Zimbabwe, and northeast of the Okavango to the central parts of northern Namibia. The pale grey bark flakes to reveal creamish-yellow new bark, and the twigs lack lenticels. The leaves are elliptic with many obscure lateral veins.

Notes

- Ochnas make interesting garden subjects because their new spring leaves can be bronze to pale greenish-yellow, their flowers are showy and the fruits can persist for several months. The widely cultivated, indigenous Carnival ochna (*O. serrulata*) has become a rather invasive shrub.

Coco-plum Family

Chrysobalanaceae

~525 spp. globally; ~2 spp. regionally, 1 spp. of tree

BW

Large mobola-plum twigs and flowers. Both the tiny cream flowers and the outer parts of young twigs are covered in velvety brown hairs.

A rather indistinct family having:

- ✓ leaves that are simple, spirally arranged, with entire margins
- ✓ stipules
- ✓ fleshy fruits with a single seed

In our region, the only tree-sized member of this family is the **Large mobola-plum** (*Parinari curatellifolia*), which is fairly distinctive, being medium to large and evergreen, with a spreading mushroom-shaped canopy. These trees often grow on sandy soils in open bushveld and occur widely in Mpumalanga, the grasslands of central Zimbabwe, and in northern Botswana and Caprivi. The leaves (30–70 mm) are matt, dark green above and white-buff below, with lateral veins in a herringbone pattern. The ovoid fruits (50 × 35 mm) are diagnostic, having a tough, white-spotted grey skin that ripens to yellow.

WT

Large mobola-plums can have a dense funnel-shaped canopy. They often grow on sandy soils derived from granite. ***Inset top:*** Note the slightly zigzagging twig and herringbone pattern of the lateral veins. Both twigs and leaves are covered with velvety brown hairs. ***Inset bottom:*** Details of the leaf under-surface, showing the conspicuous venation and tiny, woolly white hairs.

WT

Notes

- Because the fruits are prized by local people, Large mobola-plums are often not chopped down and remain dotted through the landscape.
- The similar Small mobola-plum (*P. capensis*) occurs in damp grasslands in northeastern KwaZulu-Natal and southern Mozambique. This low shrub resprouts regularly after fire. It was once incorrectly believed to be a form of the Large mobola-plum.

ML

Large mobola-plum leaves are stiffish and bicoloured, with herringbone venation. The twigs zigzag slightly and the mature fruits are brown and speckled.

Mangosteen Family

Clusiaceae

~1 610 spp. globally; ~10 spp. regionally, ~3 spp. of tree

The family has some fairly distinctive features:

✓ opposite, entire leaves
✓ yellow latex

African mangosteens (*Garcinia livingstonei*) are small to medium-sized trees, with rigid twigs that grow at right angles to the branches. The stiff, leathery, matt leaves (40–110 mm) are roundish and are borne in whorls of three. The almost spherical fruit (to 25 mm) is orange when ripe and has a tough skin. Despite the thick yellowish latex the fruit is delicious. These trees grow at low altitudes in open bushveld and riverine areas from northern KwaZulu-Natal to Beira in the lowveld. They also occur in the Zambezi valley.

Forest mangosteens (*G. gerrardii*) range in size from shrubs to small trees. The leaves are opposite (40–90 mm), leathery and glossy above. The petioles are acutely angled. These trees are found in shaded positions in coastal or afromontane forest from the northern parts of the Eastern Cape through KwaZulu-Natal and along the Lebombo Mountains.

GN

Female **African mangosteen** flowers occur more sparsely than male flowers.

GN

African mangosteens bear their leaves on stout twigs, in whorls of three. Young leaves are a russet colour.

NC

The young leaves of a **Forest mangosteen** are pale bronze. Note the opposite arrangement and the point at which the petioles attach to the stem.

Forest mangosteens have pale, smoothish, mottled bark ***(left)*** and elliptical fruit with a pointed tip ***(right)***.

GN

African mangosteens bear fruits of various ages on old wood. The ripe fruits have tough, smooth orange skin.

Willow Family

Salicaceae

~800 spp. globally; ~30 spp. regionally, ~20 spp. of tree

CV

Kei-apple sourberry in full fruit. Note the leaf clusters. *Inset:* The leaves are clustered on dwarf shoots.

This is not an easy family to classify vegetatively and DNA studies have lumped together a number of genera previously in a variety of families. However, these woody species all have the following features:

- ✓ simple leaves, with stipules
- ✓ leaves usually alternate and margins often serrate
- ✓ the marginal serrations have a vein that ends in an apical structure (look carefully with a ×10 lens)
- ✓ inner bark fibrous

Within the region the sourberry genus is the largest in the willow family, with ~8 species. Most sourberries have spines as well as leaves that are in bunches on dwarf branches. Three or more veins start from the leaf base, although the two lateral veins may be difficult to see.

Kei-apple sourberries (*Dovyalis caffra*) are probably the best known because they were extensively planted by early European colonists as hedges and to provide fruit. These shrubs or small trees occur in bushveld, on forest edges and along streams near the coast. They are found from Knysna to northern KwaZulu-Natal, and along the Lebombo Mountains into southern Zimbabwe.

Apricot sourberries (*D. zeyheri*) are small slender trees found in bushveld, often in rocky areas, from Knysna northwards just below the escarpment to the Limpopo River, and as far west as Mahikeng. They are also found in central and eastern Zimbabwe. They are distinguished from Kei-apple sourberries by having thinner leaves with serrate margins and less robust spines, as well as much smaller fruits: 10–20 rather than 30–50 mm long.

Cumquin sourberries (*D. rhamnoides*) occur from Mossel Bay to the Lebombo Mountains, usually in forest. Their leaves are mostly single and the margins more evenly serrate.

BW

Apricot sourberries have separate male and female trees. The mass of anthers indicates that these are male flowers.

Apricot sourberry leaves are typically slightly hairy, with scalloped margins.

GN

Cumquin sourberry leaves are shiny and rounded with slightly scalloped margins. Note the spines.

Rough under-surface of **Cumquin sourberry** leaf with even serrations.

Notes

- All these *Dovyalis* spp. have edible fruits.
- They all have a generic look that will enable you to identify them easily. Look for the glossy to matt leaves, mostly in clusters, occasional long and sharp spines, and a fairly straggly, untidy look.

Scolopia comprises five tree species that are east coast forest or bushveld specialists. All have simple, alternate, leathery, glossy leaves, mostly with neatly serrate margins.

Waxy thorn-pears (*S. zeyheri*) are the most widespread *Scolopia* species. They occur from Knysna to northern KwaZulu-Natal, into Botswana northwest of Mahikeng, and in parts of central and eastern Zimbabwe. These small to medium-sized trees are characterised by the robust branched spines that occur on the trunk. Unfortunately, these spines are not universal, but when present are diagnostic – together with the narrow to almost round leaves that, when gently folded and unfolded, turn whitish as the waxy leaf surface (cuticle) lifts.

Cockspur red-pears (*S. mundii*) may attain heights of 15 m in forest habitats, but are generally smaller. Their presence in an area is best indicated by the numerous seedlings and saplings in the subcanopy. These small plants have many long thin spines and glossy quilted leaves with sharply toothed margins. Up in the canopy spines are rare and the leaves are not as glossy, quilted or serrate. This tree occurs in afromontane forest from Cape Town to the northern Drakensberg and west of Gauteng.

Large-leaved brown-ironwoods (*Homalium dentatum*) are large afromontane forest trees found from Port St Johns to the northern Drakensberg and in the highlands of Zimbabwe. They also occur on forest edges and in woody ravines. The leaves are almost round (40–100 mm) with lateral veins that look indented above, conspicuously raised below. There are hairy pockets on the leaf undersurface. The margins are generally evenly serrate.

Large-leaved wild-mulberries (*Trimeria grandifolia*) occur in similar areas to brown-ironwoods and are closely allied to them, but are distinguished by their much smaller size and bigger, circular leaves (60–150 mm), which have a drip-tip and 5–7 veins from the base.

EvJ (incl. inset)

The robust branched spines on the trunk of the **Waxy thorn-pear** are diagnostic. ***Inset:*** The leaves are stiff and conspicuously serrated and the spines can be robust.

The serrations of the young and coppice leaves of the **Cockspur red-pear** have spiny tips to them. ***Inset:*** The leaves of young plants are paler and less glossy below.

TA

Large-leaved brown-ironwoods typically have almost round leaves with reddish-brown petioles.

Large-leaved wild-mulberries have nearly round leaves with 5–7 basal veins, a tiny drip-tip and evenly serrate margins.

Notes

- The remaining *Scolopia* spp. tend to be slender, small to medium-sized, with neat leaves. They grow in higher altitude forest.
- Brown-ironwoods and Wild-mulberries have 'twins' that are shrubs or small trees with smaller, more elliptic leaves. Both occur from East London into KwaZulu-Natal, usually on forest edges or rocky outcrops. These are the Small-leaved brown-ironwood (*Homalium rufescens*) and Small-leaved wild-mulberry (*Trimeria trinervis*).

HFG

The **African snuff-box tree** gets the scientific specific name *spinosa* from its stout spines.

African snuff-box trees (*Oncoba spinosa*) are spiny shrubs and small trees that have quilted leaves (30–100 mm) with finely serrate margins. They bear persistent fruits (50–60 mm round) that are dark reddish-brown when ripe and turn black with age. The showy white flowers are large (~90 mm in diameter) and have a central mass of yellow stamens. They occur from the Lebombo Mountains into the lowveld, in the Zambezi valley and in the vicinity of Maputo.

There is just one indigenous species of willow in the region, the **African willow** (*Salix mucronata*). It is highly variable and many subtypes are recognised. This bush or small tree occurs in rocky positions on the banks of permanent or semi-permanent streams and rivers. The branches are generally upright, but on large and old trees they may droop a little. The leaves are highly variable, but are usually far narrower than they are long, light green and a little glossy above and bluish below, with neatly serrate margins.

The green fruits of the **African snuff-box tree** turn reddish-brown and then black when ripe and are used to make curios.

TA

The big showy flowers of the **African snuff-box tree** have a large central cluster of yellow stamens.

EvJ

Male **African willow** flowers are cylindrical 'catkins', typical of willows globally. ***Inset:*** The leaves are long, narrow and bicoloured.

Notes

- Stripped African willow bark can be used as string and the thin twigs in basketry.
- Old African snuff-box fruits are sometimes filled with pebbles and then used as musical instruments.

INTRODUCED SPECIES: The **Weeping willow** (*Salix babylonica*) is an introduced deciduous species that occurs widely along streams and river banks. It has long, leafy, hanging branches and long, thin, glossy leaves that are pale green above and bluish below, with finely serrate margins.

Poplars also belong to the willow family and several species have become invasive locally, particularly along rivers at higher altitudes. Propagation takes place mainly from root suckers, so poplars tend to occur in groves.

Weeping willows are graceful trees that occur along waterways. They lose their leaves in winter.

Wild-peach Family

Achariaceae

~150 spp. globally; 3 spp. regionally, ~3 spp. of tree

The three genera in this family, each with only one, or a few, species, have few vegetative diagnostic features; but each species discussed is not difficult to identify.

- ✓ leaves are simple
- ✓ margins are generally serrate

African forest-peaches (*Rawsonia lucida*) are forest subcanopy trees found from Port St Johns to the northern Drakensberg, as well as from eastern Zimbabwe to Beira in Mozambique. They generally occur in warmer environments. The smooth mottled bark peels in patches to reveal orange underbark. Add to this the highly glossy stiffish leaves (60–120 mm) with spiky margins and the species is readily identifiable.

African dog-roses (*Xylotheca kraussiana*) are small forest-edge trees in coastal areas from about Port St Johns to north of Maputo. The broadly elliptic leaves (60–100 mm) are dark green and a little glossy above, and dull and much paler below, with a yellowish midrib and veins. The margins are entire and slightly rolled under. The flowers are similar to those of the African snuff-box tree, just a little smaller and generally more abundant. The fruit is an ovoid woody capsule 30–40 mm long.

African wild-peaches (*Kiggelaria africana*) can grow to be large trees, but are more often small. They occur in many habitats, including forest, forest edges, rocky and riparian areas, and ravines. They are widespread, can be locally common and are found in a broad band from the Western Cape through the Eastern Cape, KwaZulu-Natal, Limpopo and North West provinces, as well as in the eastern districts of Zimbabwe. Some leaves are small (30–50 mm), olive-green with woolly under-surfaces and entire margins; others are large (120–180 mm), pale green and thinly textured with softly spiky margins. However, the hairy pockets in the axils of the veins on the under-surface are a characteristic feature, as are the round, sub-woody, greyish fruits (15–30 mm), which open into a flattish star, revealing the fleshy orange layer covering the seeds.

The leaves of the **African forest-peach** are glossy and stiff with spiky serrations. ***Inset:*** The petiole twists slightly. Note the clear stipular scar (see arrow) and marginal spikes.

BW

An open fruit of the **African dog-rose.** The fruits are ovoid woody capsules 30–40 mm long.

GG

African dog-rose flowers are sweet-smelling.

There is no mistaking an **African wild-peach** in fruit. The warty greenish-yellowish capsules split open into star-shaped structures. ***Inset left:*** The leaf under-surface is whitish and woolly. Note the tiny pockets in the axils of the secondary veins. ***Inset right:*** The leaf upper-surface has a finely cobbled texture and 'blisters' in the axils of the secondary veins indicating the pockets below.

Notes

- African wild-peaches can be defoliated by a larva that is toxic to all birds except cuckoos.
- African dog-roses grow well in frost-free gardens.

Caper Family

Capparaceae

~700 spp. globally; ~50 spp. regionally, ~15 spp. of tree

Kudu and giraffe have browsed on this **White-trunked shepherds-tree**, giving the canopy its funnel-like shape. Note that the pruned foliage is tightly packed. ***Inset:*** The leaves are often in small bunches on short shoots and the fruits are green and hairy.

EvJ

An unusually large **Kaoko shepherds-tree** – the relatively straight under-edge marks the browse line.

Many of these mostly tropical species are not easily identified without flowers and/or fruits. However, the following are important family characteristics:

- ✓ flowers are usually conspicuous with many long powder puff-like stamens, and the ovary is on a distinctive long stalk (gynophore) that is most obvious when the tree is bearing young fruits
- ✓ usually small, even squat, evergreen trees
- ✓ leaves are alternate, though in some species they occur in tight clusters
- ✓ leaves can be simple, trifoliolate or palmate

One member of this family that is fairly easy to identify is the **White-trunked shepherds-tree** (*Boscia albitrunca*) – known as *Witgat* in Afrikaans, because of the whitish trunk. This species is widespread in bushveld vegetation and is quite variable, seldom attaining a height of over 4 m. It has a dense, hemispherical, dark green canopy that is often well browsed, appearing tightly pruned with a straight under-edge in areas that are browsed by cattle and goats. The stocky whitish trunk can be fluted. The small simple leaves (generally <30 mm) usually occur in tight clusters on thickish, spine-like twigs.

Kaoko shepherds-trees (*B. microphylla*) occur in northwestern Namibia. They are spiny shrubs or medium-sized trees that often occur on rocky mountain slopes. The blue-green leaves distinguish them from the Stink shepherds-trees.

The **Stink shepherds-tree** (*B. foetida*) has two recognisable forms. One form occurs in the west, in bushveld and karoo areas from the Northern Cape to the Cunene River, and the other in bushveld from central Botswana into northern South Africa and southern Zimbabwe. Both forms have small leaves (<15 mm) and occasional spine-tipped twigs. The bark is mostly brown, but can be whitish and is then easily confused with the White-trunked shepherds-tree.

GN

Stink shepherds-tree flowers are not the big powder puffs typical of the family, but are somewhat reduced.

When **Stink shepherds-trees** have white bark, they may be confused with White-trunked shepherds-trees. However their bark is rougher and the trunk less fluted.

The bead-beans are mostly shrubs or small trees.

The **Bushveld bead-bean** (*Maerua angolensis*) occurs at lower altitudes in eastern bushveld areas from southern KwaZulu-Natal to the Zambezi. The trunk is light grey to brown and smooth. The simple leaves are thinly textured with a leaf stalk almost as long as the leaf blade (the whole length being 25–60 mm). There is no mistaking the 'beaded bean' fruits.

The **Ringwood bead-bean** (*M. schinzii*) is superficially similar to the Bushveld bead-bean, but it is a western bushveld species found in Namibia. The biggest difference between the two is that the Namibian species has leathery, sometimes velvety, yellow-green leaves.

African cucumber-bushes (*Thilachium africanum*) are small trees found at low altitude in the bushveld, from Swaziland northwards to the Zambezi. The leaves are simple or trifoliolate, leathery, with a sunken yellowish midrib (40–160 mm), characteristically prominent veins, and margins that are somewhat rolled under. The fruit, a woody 'pod' up to 60 mm long, has 12 distinct ribs.

Bushveld bead-bean flowers. A family feature is the gynophore – a stalked ovary that extends clear of the flower.

GN

Bushveld bead-beans are named for their characteristic beaded fruits that may be produced *en masse*.

BW

BW

JB

Left: The generally trifoliolate leaves of the **African cucumber-bush** are tough, leathery and have conspicuous veins that are a little wavy. *Centre:* The species gets its common name from the fruits, which resemble ribbed cucumbers. *Right:* The powder-puff flowers are typical of the family. Note the stiff leaves, conspicuous veins and sharp mucro.

Notes

- Lianas (*Capparis* spp.) are the most conspicuous plants in this family as they flower prolifically. Many lianas have pairs of tiny, very tough and sharp recurved spines.

Myrrh Family

Burseraceae

~540 spp. globally; ~34 spp. regionally, 25 spp. of tree

EvJ

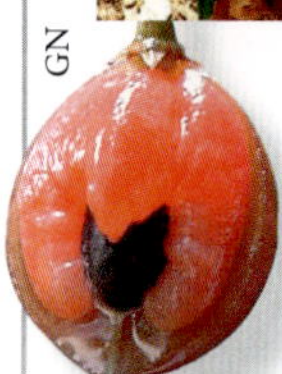

GN

Corkwoods often have peeling papery bark. One of the most spectacular examples is the **Copper-stemmed corkwood (*above*)**. Its seeds are also typical of the family, being covered by a reddish fleshy aril **(*left*)**.

A single genus represents the myrrh family in the region. *Commiphora* spp. have the following features:

- ✓ small to medium-sized, mostly confined to dry bushveld and semi-desert
- ✓ strongly aromatic leaves smell a little like turpentine when crushed
- ✓ visible, cloudy (rarely milky) latex can be difficult to see in dry periods
- ✓ seeds are usually covered by a yellowish to bright red and fleshy aril
- ✓ leaves are pinnately compound or trifoliolate, rarely simple
- ✓ generally smooth bark that peels off in large papery pieces

The following trees in this family have papery bark and pinnately compound leaves:

The **Copper-stemmed corkwood** (*C. harveyi*) usually has pinnately compound (sometimes trifoliolate) leaves and occurs in tall dry bushveld and scrub forest at low altitudes from East London to the Kruger National Park.

Paperbark corkwoods (*C. marlothii*) are similar to Copper-stemmed corkwoods but the bark is green, sloughing off in large, floppy, papery sheets. They generally occur in rocky sites north of the Soutpansberg to the Zambezi valley in Zimbabwe.

The following trees have pinnately compound leaves and bark that peels off in small flakes:

Found in bushveld and thicket vegetation, the **Rough-leaved corkwood** (*C. edulis*) grows on rocky sites in the Zambezi and Limpopo valleys.

The pinnately compound leaves of the **Paperbark corkwood** typically occur in terminal clusters. ***Inset:*** The bark sloughs off in large papery sheets.

HFG

Rough-leaved corkwoods have pinnately compound leaves. Note the single fruit.

Velvet-leaved corkwoods (*C. mollis*) have silvery to light brown bark that peels off in small flakes. The species also occurs on rocky sites in hot dry bushveld from north of Swaziland and Kimberley through Zimbabwe to the Zambezi, and in Kaokoland.

The **Forest corkwood** (*C. woodii*) is one of the few species that does not have peeling bark. It is a forest tree with mostly pinnately compound leaves. It occurs from Port St Johns to the Mozambiquan border, and inland almost to the border of Lesotho.

Trees with simple or trifoliolate leaves that have smooth bark, and are not spinescent, include the following:

Sand corkwoods (*C. angolensis*) can have up to five leaflets. As the name implies their ideal habitat is Kalahari sand from the North West province westwards into Namibia and Kaokoland.

The **Pepper-leaved corkwood** (*C. mossambicensis*) is restricted largely to Zimbabwe where it occurs in hot, dry, rocky habitats. The twigs have dense, velvety, glandular golden hairs.

Satin-bark corkwoods (*C. tenuipetiolata*) have smooth pale grey to bluish bark that peels off in silvery to pale yellow pieces. This species is generally hairless. It occurs in central and northern Namibia in dry bushveld, with a disjunct population in the central Limpopo valley.

JB

The starkly pale bark of the **Satin-bark corkwood** makes it conspicuous in dry bushveld. ***Inset:*** Note the long petiole of this trifoliolate leaf.

BW

Velvet-leaved corkwoods have softly hairy leaflets, from which they get their common name.

EvJ

Forest corkwoods carry their fruits and bunches of leaves at the twig ends.

HFG

Sand corkwoods can be many-stemmed. Note the brownish lenticels.

BW

The fine hairs of the **Pepper-leaved corkwood** are soon lost. Note the long petioles and broad leaflets.

Notes

- Corkwoods are not always easy to identify and in recent years a few new species have been discovered in semi-arid regions such as northern Namibia. Today there is a small but lucrative cottage industry in Kaokoland where people collect corkwood gum for use in the cosmetics industry.
- Species in this family are the source of myrrh and of frankincense.

Simple leaves of the **Tall firethorn corkwood**. Some corkwoods have simple leaves and may even have simple and trifoliolate leaves on the same plant. Note the stout spine.

The remaining corkwoods are spinescent, have simple and/or trifoliolate leaves and smooth bark:

Tall firethorn corkwoods (*C. glandulosa*) occur on sandy sites and in mopane country. They are found in a wide belt across the northern part of the region and extend south down to the Lebombo Mountains and KwaZulu-Natal. They are densely twiggy small trees.

Sweet-root corkwoods (*C. neglecta*) are similar. They have green trunks and often occur in small groves. They are found in bushveld vegetation in Limpopo, through the Kruger National Park and its environs southwards into central KwaZulu-Natal.

Glossy-leaved corkwoods (*C. schimperi*) have leaflets with quite coarsely toothed margins. They occur in central Zimbabwe, through the North West province, Limpopo and Mpumalanga and into central KwaZulu-Natal.

JB

Sometimes the bark below the papery peelings is quite smooth and green, as is the case with this **Sweet-root corkwood**.

Some corkwoods, like this **Sweet-root corkwood,** have trifoliolate leaves. Note the prominent yellowish midrib.

HFG

HFG

HFG

Left: Corkwoods rarely have regular bark. However, one species that does is the **Forest corkwood**. *Centre:* The bark of the **Rough-leaved corkwood** peels off in tiny furry bits. *Right:* The bark of the **Glossy-leaved corkwood** peels off in tiny flakes.

Mango Family

Anacardiaceae 500 spp. globally; >80 spp. regionally, ~70 spp. of tree

Regionally this is the fourth largest tree family. Most species in this extremely diverse family are shrubs and small trees. Although individual genera are easy to identify, family characteristics are less obvious, other than the following:

- ✓ crushed leaves can have a strong turpentine or resinous smell
- ✓ stipules are absent
- ✓ several members have alternate, trifoliolate or imparipinnate leaves
- ✓ a watery or resinous exudate can be found – sometimes with difficulty
- ✓ flowers are small, inconspicuous and unisexual (male and female flowers sometimes occurring on different trees)

The **African marula** (*Sclerocarya birrea*) is an easily identifiable, medium to large, deciduous tree. It is widespread, but usually scattered, growing on sandy soils in the bushveld, from KwaZulu-Natal, through eastern Botswana, westwards along the Cunene River and eastwards to the Atlantic Ocean. The leaves are crowded on fattish twigs with 9–17 leaflets and each leaflet has a long stalk. Leaflets are pale and bluish-green below and have entire margins, except on coppice shoots and saplings. The apex is broadly tapering and the rachis pink-tinged.

Lanneas are also medium-sized bushveld trees. The **False-marula lannea** (*Lannea schweinfurthii*), which resembles the African marula, occurs in tall bushveld, usually on sandy soils or termitaria, from northern KwaZulu-Natal to the Zambezi as far as Victoria Falls and westwards to the eastern highlands. The 3–13 leaflets are almost circular, with a blunt apex. Young leaflets are hairy.

The bark of the **False-marula lannea** is quite similar to that of the African marula but the flakes are bigger and more angular. ***Inset:*** The leaflets lack the long petioles that are so typical of an African marula.

The bark of the **African marula** is mottled and exfoliates leaving shallow pale scars. ***Inset:*** Twig and green fruits. Note the pinnately compound leaves. Each leaflet has a long stalk and a finely pointed drip-tip.

Notes

- African marulas are arguably the trees most valued by South African rural communities. Not only is the fruit prized for its high Vitamin C content, but it is fermented to make a strong alcoholic beverage. The kernels are then cracked (with great difficulty, as they are extremely hard) to yield an excellent nut that is rich in oil and protein. The leaves are eaten by lepidopteron larvae, which are, in turn, gathered for food. The wood is used to make wooden bowls and spoons.
- Beetle larvae in dead African marula wood are a woodpecker's delight. In the lowveld, elephants come from afar, smashing branches to get at both the fruit and the leaves. They also de-bark individual trees. Most animals utilise this species and in some regions there seems to be little regeneration because of over-use.
- Claims that an aqueous extract of the African marula's bark possesses, among other things, analgesic and anti-inflammatory properties have been verified experimentally.
- A commercially available liqueur is made from the fruit of the African marula tree.

BW

The leaflets of the **Live-long lannea** are distinctly bicoloured and are therefore quite easy to identify.

The leaves of the **African wild-plum** are produced in characteristic terminal swirls. *Inset:* Close-up of plum-like fruits.

Notes

- Some non-indigenous species within this family have edible fruits – mangoes for example – or edible nuts, like cashews and pistachios.
- Eating greenish mangoes can result in mango sores, which resemble cold sores. They occur in the corners of the mouth and spread down on either side of the chin. The burning is caused by turpinoids.

Another fairly widespread species, the **Live-long lannea** (*L. discolor*) is identified by its greyish leaflet undersurfaces. It has a similar distribution to the former species.

African wild-plums (*Harpephyllum caffrum*) are medium-sized to large trees found from Port Elizabeth northwards and below the escarpment to the Soutpansberg. They usually occur in forest, scrub forest, along river banks or on forest edges, especially at lower altitudes. They are readily identified by the pinnately compound leaves with asymmetric, distinctly sickle-shaped, leaflets. The leaves are clustered on twig apices that look swirled. Occasional red leaflets or leaves are also characteristic.

A number of small to medium, rarely large, trees in the family have simple leaves with herringbone venation:

The biggest tree in this group is the **Forest red-beech** (*Protorhus longifolia*), which is a coastal forest tree found from about East London to northern KwaZulu-Natal, and then along the Lebombo Mountains to the Soutpansberg. Ideal habitat includes forest edges, riparian areas and rocky forest sites. Distinctive characteristics are the occasional old red leaf in the canopy, the longish petioles (up to 25 mm) and the lateral veins, which branch just before the margins.

The **Cape rockwood** (*Heeria argentea*) is a distinctive small, gnarled stocky tree, found on rocky outcrops in fynbos.

Typically the young leaves of the **Forest red-beech** are reddish and held upright (occasional old leaves are also red). *Inset:* Mature leaf showing the herringbone venation pattern. Note that the veins branch just before the translucent margin.

EvJ

Cape rockwoods are readily identified by their very stiff leaves, the herringbone venation pattern, and the translucent yellowish veins.

All the remaining species in this group are resin-trees, which can be divided into two types: those with leaves that are alternate and spirally arranged, and those that have opposite or three-whorled leaves. The following two species fall into the former group:

Namibian resin-trees (*Ozoroa crassinervia*) occur from the Northern Cape through central and western Namibia to the Cunene River. They are small trees found in stony and rocky arid bushveld sites. The broad leaves are clustered towards the twig apices and have a felty grey under-surface.

The **Tarberry resin-tree** (*O. reticulata*) of Zimbabwe also occurs in bushveld vegetation on the northern border between Botswana and Namibia. The leaves are narrow, mostly with a tapering apex and a mucro. The twigs and leaf under-surfaces are densely covered with matted yellowish to rust-coloured hairs. This is quite a variable species but the net-veining is always conspicuous (hence the scientific name *reticulata*).

The following resin-trees have opposite or three-whorled leaves:

The **Drooping resin-tree** (*O. engleri*) is a stout shrub or small tree. The leaves, as the common name suggests, are drooping. They are thinly textured, grey-green above, glossy silver and hairy below. The petioles can be pinkish. This species is found in low-altitude bushveld, often on sand or on rocky hills from northern KwaZulu-Natal to southern Mozambique, along the Lebombo Mountains.

The **Bushveld resin-tree** (*O. paniculosa*) is much more widespread. It occurs in rocky bushveld from KwaZulu-Natal through to northern Namibia. The leaves tend to be long and slender, bicoloured, with a wavy margin and a rounded apex.

Bushveld resin-tree showing the petioles attached in whorls on a twig.

WS (incl. inset)

Namibian resin-trees are small and gnarled and grow in rocky areas. ***Inset:*** The stiff, hairy leaves have a slightly wavy margin.

BW

The leaves of the **Tarberry resin-tree** are thickish and are covered with sparse yellowish hairs.

HFG

The **Drooping resin-tree** takes its name from the drooping habit of its leaves. They are whorled and have an attenuated tip.

The easiest *Searsia* to identify is the **Red currant** because of its large pendulous leaves and reddish twigs. The leaves have wavy margins. ***Inset:*** *Searsia* flowers are generally tiny, pale, and occur in bunches.

Members of the genus *Searsia* (formerly *Rhus* spp.) all have trifoliolate leaves that are highly variable within and between species. Many are extremely difficult to identify.

The largest tree in the region is the **Red currant** (*S. chirindensis*), which is medium-sized, rarely large, and found in a wide variety of moist habitats, from mountainsides and forests to open bushveld. They occur from about Swellendam and in a band below the escarpment onto the Lebombo and Chimanimani mountains. Short spine-like twigs are often characteristic, as well as the large, pendulous, pale green leaves, which have long petioles (up to 170 mm) and tapering, almost hair-like, tips.

Arguably the most widespread and conspicuous *Searsia* is the **Lance-leaved karee** (*S. lancea*). The leaves are pendulous, comprising olive-green leaflets that are very narrow, sometimes glossy and resinous, with tight lateral veins and entire margins. This small to medium tree is widespread in inland bushveld and riverine situations throughout southern Africa, excluding Botswana.

The similar **White karee** (*S. pendulina*) has more thinly textured leaves. This riverbank specialist occurs along the Orange River. Today it is widely cultivated and can be difficult to identify because of hybridisation.

Another very similar species is the **Mountain karee** (*S. leptodictya*), which is distinguished from the previous two species by the serrate leaflet margins.

Left: **Lance-leaved karees** are identified by their long, slender, tapering, toughish leaflets. In spring they bear masses of flowers. ***Centre:*** **White karee** leaflets have more rounded tips than those of the Lance-leaved karee. ***Right:*** **Mountain karees** look similar to Lance-leaved karees but the leaf margins are distinctly finely serrate.

The **Blue-fruit currant** (*S. crenata*) is fairly easy to identify. It is a shrub or many-branched small tree that grows along the coast from Cape Town almost as far as Durban. It has small, neatly serrate, glossy, sometimes leathery and stiffish leaflets that are rounded. The margins roll under.

The **Crowberry currant** (*S. pentheri*) is a small neat bushveld tree, but also occurs in thornveld and scrub, from Grahamstown northwards into Limpopo (but never on sandy soils). The leaves are thinly textured, with dark green upper-surfaces and much paler under-surfaces. The leaflets are hairy when young.

The **Blunt-leaved currant** (*S. rehmanniana*) is a small tree of thicket and high-rainfall grasslands, and occurs from Cape Town to the northern Lebombo Mountains. The leaflets are rather leathery and quilted, with blunt apices.

The leaflets of the **Blue fruit currant** are neatly rounded with small serrations and are held in quite tight apical bunches.

ML

The leaves of the **Crowberry currant** are somewhat hairy with a few apical serrations.

Blunt-leaved currants fruit in profusion. ***Inset:*** They have rather leathery, quilted leaflets, with blunt apices.

INTRODUCED SPECIES: Two South American members of the mango family, the **Brazilian pepper** (*Schinus terebinthifolius*) and the **Pepper tree** (*S. molle*), are becoming invasive, the former in KwaZulu-Natal and northwards, and the latter in arid regions. Both grow easily and are often cultivated. Birds disperse their seeds.

Pepper trees have willow-like, hanging, pinnately compound leaves and twigs.

Brazilian pepper fruits and leaves. Birds disperse the seeds of this invasive species.

Notes

- Recent DNA studies have shown that what we used to call *Rhus* in the region more correctly belongs to the genus *Searsia*. Not only are many *Searsia* spp. difficult to identify (even for professionals), but the taxonomic status, not just at the species level but also at the genus level, is complex. Changing the scientific name of a plant is always problematic and in some cases common names have been more stable than scientific ones!
- Some people have allergic reactions to *Searsia* spp., which are close allies to species like Poison-ivy in North America and *Lithraea caustica* from South America. (The specific name *caustica* refers to the caustic nature of the leaves.)

Litchi family

Sapindaceae

~2 000 spp. globally; ~30 spp. regionally, all trees

There are 19 genera in the family regionally and most can be identified by a combination of the following features:

- ✓ alternate leaves, without stipules
- ✓ three species have simple leaves, 8 have leaves with two or three leaflets, and the remainder are pinnately compound
- ✓ those with pinnately compound leaves, generally have <11 pairs of opposite to sub-opposite leaflets (one species is bipinnate)

The **Bushveld jacket-plum** (*Pappea capensis*) is a small to medium-sized tree that is often heavily browsed. It has variable simple leaves with margins that are either entire or, more often, finely toothed. Occasionally they are coarsely toothed, especially on young plants and coppice growth. The leaves are usually crowded apically, and are leathery, rough (seemingly unable to 'lie flat'), dull green above and noticeably paler below. The venation is characteristic – the many parallel veins divide close to the leaf margin. Leaf size is also highly variable, from 20–160 mm. The species is easily identified by these leaf characteristics despite its vegetative variability. The fruits are furry green capsules (~15 mm) with a shiny black seed completely surrounded by a bright orange-red fleshy cover. Arguably the most widespread tree in the family, it occurs in many habitats from Karoo hill slopes to rocky outcrops in the east, and on riparian fringes and termitaria in bushveld. It is absent only from grassland, the Kalahari and Namibia.

African sand-olives (*Dodonaea viscosa*) also have simple leaves and occur as shrubs or small slender trees, often in groves, on sandy substrates in many dryish habitats. They extend from the Western Cape eastwards through the Little Karoo and along the coastal belt to Swaziland, then west as far as Kimberley and northwards to the Zambezi. Characteristically, the narrowly elliptic pale green leaves have a resinous and sticky surface when young. The two- to three-winged fruit measures ~15 mm.

LL

▲ The flowers of the **Bushveld jacket-plum** are small and yellowish. Note that the leaves do not lie flat and, in this specimen, have almost entire margins.

▲ The leaves on the coppice shoots and saplings of the **Bushveld jacket-plum** may have conspicuously serrate margins.

GN

▲ Ripe fruit of the **Bushveld jacket-plum**. The brown 'jacket' has split open, revealing the plum-coloured fruit.

The papery-winged fruits and narrow resinous leaves of the **African sand-olive** are diagnostic. ***Inset:*** Detail of the leaf upper-surface. Close inspection would reveal tiny resinous lumps. ▶

False-currants are easily distinguished from currants (*Searsia* spp.) by the fact that their trifoliolate leaves lack the faint resinous smell when crushed.

The **African false-currant** (*Allophylus africanus*) is the most widespread of the species with trifoliolate leaves. It occurs from north of East London to the Lebombo Mountains, from the coast to the escarpment and also from the Zambezi mouth westwards through northern Zimbabwe to the Caprivi Strip and along the Cunene River. This small tree is found in bushveld, frequently on termitaria and in riparian bush. A key distinguishing characteristic is that the looping lateral veins on the leaflets end in marginal teeth.

The **Small-leaved false-currant** (*A. decipiens*) occurs from Knysna to the Lebombo Mountains and is distinguished from the African false-currant by having looping lateral veins and pockets that are conspicuous on all three leaflets (whereas in the former species the pockets tend to be concentrated on the central leaflet).

Dune false-currants (*A. natalensis*) are small trees found at the edges of dune forest from East London to north of Maputo. The lateral veins end at the leaflet margins as in the previous two species, but the leaflets tend to be more narrowly elliptic, largely lack hairy pockets and have scalloped rather than serrate margins. A conspicuous trait is the mass of small red fruits (~7 mm), which can weigh down the branches.

One widespread common species that has pinnately compound leaves is the **False perdepis** (*Hippobromus pauciflorus*). It is found mostly in coastal regions from Knysna to the Lebombo Mountains, below the escarpment. It is a densely leafy small tree of riparian thicket and dry forest edges, and has a conspicuously winged rachis.

False perdepis leaf photographed against the tree trunk. Note the deeply serrate leaflets and winged rachis.

CV

GN

African false-currant with typical flowering spike comprising tiny white flowers. ***Inset:*** The looping lateral veins end in serrations.

EvJ

Small-leaved false-currant with fruits. Close examination would reveal tiny lumps on the leaf upper-surface, indicating that there are pockets in the axils of the veins below.

AS

Twigs of the **Dune false-currant** showing the narrowish, neatly serrate leaves and short petioles. ***Inset:*** Note the venation and tiny hairy pockets in the leaf under-surface.

Notes

- Bushveld jacket-plums are characteristic small trees of the Little Karoo. They are heavily browsed, which gives them a hemispherical canopy and means that they could, at first glance, be taken for Small-leaved guarris. They are an important constituent of the Addo bushveld inland of Port Elizabeth. Elsewhere they are scattered through bushveld.
- African sand-olives have a cosmopolitan distribution in subtropical and tropical areas. They make excellent hedges.
- One species of false-currant has a simple leaf, the two lateral leaves having been lost via evolution. This species, the Simple-leaved false-currant, has a petiole with two swellings (like the *Cola* spp.) and the 'simple' leaf is similar to the terminal leaflet of the African false-currant.

Velvet-fruit zanhas (*Zanha africana*) are medium-sized trees that occur on koppies and in riparian bush across northern and central Zimbabwe. The leaves are up to 150 mm long, and the undersurfaces of the leaflets are covered in light brown hairs. The roundish fruits (~30 mm) are bright orange and velvety.

The **African river-litchi** (*Lecaniodiscus fraxinifolius*) is a medium-sized tree that forms thickets along rivers and drainage lines in the Zambezi valley and along the coast from KwaZulu-Natal to north of Beira. Young leaves are reddish, turn yellowish-green and then darken with age. The fruits are roundish (up to 15 mm), velvety, and yellow to pink.

The three krantz-ash species all have woody winged fruits that tend to be held upright. The leaf rachis ends in a little extension. All have similar leaves and fruits, but since their distributions do not overlap they are easily identified by where they occur.

The **Lebombo krantz-ash** (*Atalaya alata*) occurs in scrub forest along the Lebombo Mountains and has asymmetric, slightly curved leaflets.

The **Cape krantz-ash** (*A. capensis*) is a small tree of afromontane forest and bush and occurs inland of Port Elizabeth.

The **Forest krantz-ash** (*A. natalensis*) is medium-sized and occurs in forest north of Durban.

WS

Fruits and leaflets of the **Velvet-fruit zanha**. In good years they fruit profusely.

CV

The pinnately compound, shiny and hairless leaves of an **African river-litchi** (shown against the tree trunk).

GN

Paired winged fruits and curved serrate leaflets are typical of the **Lebombo krantz-ash**.

EvJ

Cape krantz-ash fruits are similar to those of the Lebombo krantz-ash, but the leaflets are not serrate.

TA

Forest krantz-ashes have shinier, less oblique leaves than those of the two other krantz-ash species.

Notes

- Individual winged fruits behave like helicopters, dispersing the seeds a good distance from the parent plant in windy conditions.

Kirkia Family

Kirkiaceae

~6 spp. globally; 3 spp. regionally, all trees

Species in this family have the following characteristics:

- ✓ imparipinnate, spirally arranged leaves that are clustered apically and are deciduous
- ✓ leaflets are not entire
- ✓ spectacular autumn colours
- ✓ local species tend to have fattish twigs that have conspicuous leaf scars

White kirkias (*Kirkia wilmsii*) tend to grow in rocky areas in bushveld. They are small deciduous trees with a rounded canopy. They occur through much of Zimbabwe and northern Mozambique, and just into eastern Botswana and northern South Africa – with outlier communities in Kaokoland.

Mountain kirkias (*K. acuminata*) are more restricted, occurring only in northeastern South Africa. They often grow on calcium-rich, rocky bushveld sites. The leaves have more leaflet pairs (10–22 versus 6–10), and they are smaller than those of the White kirkia (6–25 mm versus 20–70 mm).

White kirkia with fresh summer foliage.

A **Mountain kirkia** in autumn. *Inset:* Typical pinnately compound leaves massed on twig ends. Note the thinly woody fruit capsules.

White kirkia leaves and tiny flowers. The foliage appears feathery.

CS

A close-up of **White kirkia** leaves in autumn colours.

Notes

- Both species tend to grow in groves, sometimes so extensive that they cover entire hillsides, providing a splendid show of colour in autumn.

Citrus Family

Rutaceae ~1 000 spp. globally; ~379 spp. regionally, ~20 spp. of tree

The flowers of the **Forest cape-chestnut** have pinkish-mauve petals that are speckled with darker dots. ***Inset:*** A characteristic of this family is that the leaves and some of the fruits have oil glands. They appear as translucent dots.

All members of the family are easily identified by the characteristics that follow:

- ✓ crushed leaves typically have a citrus-like smell (from faint to pungent)
- ✓ leaves and some fruits have 'oil glands' that look like translucent dots when held against strong light (sometimes only with a ×10 lens)
- ✓ all species (except the Forest cape-chestnut) have trifoliolate or pinnately compound, alternate leaves

A spectacular, well-known large tree in this family is the **Forest cape-chestnut** (*Calodendrum capense*), which has simple opposite leaves (60–120 mm). In spring the mass of pinkish flowers over the canopy is striking, and, unsurprisingly, the tree is cultivated locally and abroad. It occurs in forest from Swellendam to the Soutpansberg, and in Zimbabwe's eastern highlands.

Some 13 trees in the family have trifoliolate leaves. The following four are common and widespread:

Forest white-ironwoods (*Vepris lanceolata*) are the most widespread. This forest tree occurs from Swellendam northwards to Beira and west from KwaZulu-Natal into the North West province. It is readily identified by its distinctly wavy leaflet margins.

Drooping white-ironwoods (*V. reflexa*) are small trees found in dry forest and rocky hillsides near streams and rivers. They occur from Port St Johns to Beira, and inland from Swaziland to the North West province, as well as in the mid-Zambezi valley. The leaves droop and tend to curl up at the tips, and the veins are conspicuous.

The fruits of the **Forest cape-chestnut** are golf ball-sized and warty. They contain a few hard black seeds.

Another family feature is that many tree species have compound leaves. The trifoliolate leaves of this **Forest white-ironwood** have characteristically undulating margins.

Drooping white-ironwoods have tough and leathery leaflets with surface veins that are more visible from above than below. The leaflets themselves are opaque.

African wild-mandarins (*Toddaliopsis bremekampii*) are small, mostly evergreen trees found in dry forest from northern KwaZulu-Natal to the Soutpansberg and into the south of the Zimbabwean eastern highlands. The small, warty, lemon-like fruits are a distinguishing characteristic (10–15 mm).

A similar-looking species is the **Flaky-bark cherry-orange** (*Teclea gerrardii*), which has mottled grey bark that flakes off, leaving yellowish patches. It is a forest edge and thicket species found from southern KwaZulu-Natal to the Mozambiquan border. The more rounded leaflet tips distinguish this species from the **Slender cherry-orange** (*Teclea natalensis*), which has drooping leaves with tapering apices.

A number of species in the family have pinnately compound leaves:

Aniseed-scented horsewood (*Clausena anisata*), known as *Perdepis* in Afrikaans, is the most easily identified species in the family because the crushed leaves have a pungent odour. In addition, the first few leaflets (which are alternate) are much smaller than the apical leaflets, and they all tend to be asymmetric. This is a small, quite slender tree found in bushveld close to forest, on forest edges, on rocky outcrops, and along drainage lines. It occurs below the escarpment from about Mossel Bay to the Zambezi, and from Swaziland into Limpopo.

A leaf of the **Aniseed-scented horsewood**. The basal leaflets are much smaller than the apical leaflets. The surfaces are glossy and somewhat quilted.

NC

The green fruits of the **African wild-mandarin** have the rough skin more typical of cultivated citrus.

LL

HFG

Flaky-bark cherry-oranges have orange bark and a characteristic exfoliation pattern. ***Inset:*** The leaflets are rounded and are attached by their bases (sessile), distinguishing this species from the similar Slender cherry-orange.

JB

Slender cherry-orange leaflets have distinct petioles and taper towards the apex.

Notes

- Many fynbos shrubs are members of this family. Examples are buchus (*Agathosma* spp.) and the Confetti-bush (*Coleonema album*). The leaves contain volatile oils and are highly flammable, burning even when green and wet.

African sneezewoods (*Ptaeroxylon obliquum*) can be large trees when they occur in forests, but are smaller in scrub forest, in bushveld, in ravines and hilly areas, and even in sand forest. The species is distinguished by its leaves, which are paripinnate and have a slightly winged rachis. The leaflets are all much the same size and distinctly asymmetric, tending to be rectangular. Crushed leaves give off a peppery citrus smell. The trunks are also characteristic. They have smoothish pale grey bark that is shallowly fissured and yellowish in the grooves.

There are some 9 species of knobwood in the region, all of which are spinescent: there are also spine-tipped knobs on the trunk and bigger branches, and some species even have tiny spines on the under-surface of the leaf rachis.

Small knobwoods (*Zanthoxylum capense*) are small, rarely medium-sized, trees and occur in forest, riparian bush, scrub forest and on rocky outcrops. Their range extends from about Mossel Bay northwards, below the escarpment, as far as Inhambane, and from Swaziland into Gauteng, Limpopo and Mpumalanga. They also occur in Zimbabwe from the eastern highlands westwards to Bulawayo. Straight spines are typical of this species as are the ~10 leaflets arranged with the smallest at the bottom and largest at the leaf apex. The terminal leaflet is often missing.

Forest knobwoods (*Z. davyi*) can become quite large trees. They occur in forest below the escarpment from Knysna to the Soutpansberg, and in the eastern highlands of Zimbabwe. They can be distinguished from Small knobwoods by their recurved spines and bigger leaflets (20–70 × 10–40 mm).

African sneezewood bark is characteristically pale yellowish-brown and splits as it grows, revealing a light yellow interior – as can be seen above. ***Inset:*** The leaves are paripinnate, that is, they lack a terminal leaflet and the leaflets have distinctly unequal sides.

Small knobwood stems and branches may be covered in spine-tipped corky outgrowths.

There are little 'ears' (see arrow) where the leaflets join the rachis.

Detail of a **Small knobwood** leaf, showing that the leaflets are in fact smaller at the base and larger towards the apex.

Forest knobwood leaflet backlit to show the venation and marginal glands.

AS

Notes

- In the Eastern Cape and the Midlands of KwaZulu-Natal many large sneezewood trees were felled by early colonists for use as fencing posts and railway sleepers. In addition, small trees have always been prized for hut construction because they are termite resistant. However, sneezewoods are still widespread and locally common, and in prime sites grow reasonably quickly for a tree with such hard wood.

Hibiscus Family

Malvaceae

~2 300 spp. globally; ~280 spp. regionally, ~50 spp. of tree

Although this is the seventh largest tree family it contains not only the largest tree regionally (the African baobab) but also many widespread common shrubs and small trees. Characteristic features of this family (excluding the African baobab) include the following:

- ✓ leaves are simple and have at least three distinct veins from the base (except for *Cola* spp., which have two swellings on the petiole – one at the leaf base and one where the petiole attaches to the stem)
- ✓ leaves are alternate and stipulate
- ✓ tiny, star-shaped hairs can be present (×10 hand lens required) on many species

Raisins are widespread in bushveld and on forest margins – there are some 30 species, mostly shrubs and even some lianas. The following are some of the larger species:

Velvet raisins (*Grewia flava*) are widespread in bushveld throughout the southern African interior, but are absent from the Western and Eastern Cape and much of Zimbabwe. Leaves are held upright (20–65 mm) and have roughly symmetric bases and silvery hairs above and below.

Sandpaper raisins (*G. flavescens*) have, as the name implies, rough leaves, particularly on their under-surfaces. The leaves tend to be bigger than those of Velvet raisins (up to 120 mm) and are quite broad. A more tropical species, this tree occurs in northern Limpopo and the North West province, as well as in northern Mozambique and throughout Zimbabwe. It also extends across northern Botswana and Namibia.

Giant raisins (*G. hexamita*) have a rather restricted distribution. They occur from coastal KwaZulu-Natal and northwards to the Limpopo River. The leaves are almost as broad as they are long, and the bases are markedly asymmetric – almost lobed on one side.

GN

Giant raisins are named for their large hairy fruits.

Note the prominence of the veins on the under-surface of this **Giant raisin** leaf.

Velvet raisins have strongly bicoloured leaves with three distinct basal veins.

TW

Sandpaper raisin leaves have uneven saw-toothed margins and are asymmetric.

TW

Giant raisin: note the almost-lobed base of the leaf (partly obscured by the flower).

GN

Forest raisins have big hairy leaves with prominent venation. The fruit structure typifies *Grewia* spp.

GN

A typical **Forest raisin** flower. This flower structure is common to all *Grewia* spp.

GN (inset)

Grey raisin leaves are quite rectangular and have fine velvety hairs. ***Inset:*** The flowers are yellow.

Notes

- The Lagoon hibiscus is also a member of this family (see p. 17).
- Raisins have straightish pliable stems. Many species are used for making basket frames, and the fibrous bark is used for fine basketry.
- Many raisins have thinly fleshy edible fruits.

Forest raisins (*G. lasiocarpa*) grow on forest edges and in moist bushveld as bushes or small trees. The leaves are almost circular (mostly 70–90 mm) and are covered above and below with bristly, often rusty-coloured hairs. These trees occur from north of East London to northern KwaZulu-Natal.

Grey raisins (*G. monticola*) occur widely in bushveld from about Durban as far north as the Zambezi and westwards to Botswana. The leaves are roughly rectangular, asymmetric, have fine velvety golden hairs and are borne on drooping branches.

Cross-berry raisins (*G. occidentalis*) are common in karoo, grassland and bushveld areas throughout eastern South Africa as well as in forested habitat along the coast as far west as Cape Town. They also occur in southern Mozambique and in the eastern highlands of Zimbabwe. They have thinly textured light green leaves (20–70 mm), often held horizontally on twigs. Insects and mammals seek out the leaves.

The **Mallow raisin** (*G. villosa*) has broad, mostly circular, symmetric leaves (60–120 mm) with a quilted upper-surface and a hairy grey under-surface. This tree occurs in low-altitude bushveld and rocky habitat from northern Namibia into western Zimbabwe, in the Limpopo valley and along the Lebombo Mountains to the KwaZulu-Natal north coast.

EvJ

The branches of **Cross-berry raisins** are often held horizontally. ***Inset:*** The fruits are four-lobed, but some may abort, resulting in three-lobed fruit.

TW

The circular, symmetric, quilted leaf of a **Mallow raisin**.

Dombeyas are easily identified by their fairly persistent papery petals.

There are 9 species regionally, of which the **Wild-pear dombeya** (*Dombeya rotundifolia*) is the most widely distributed. It is a small, neat, evergreen tree found in valleys and on slopes in bushveld. It is most conspicuous – and unmistakable – when covered in white flowers during winter and spring. It can be found from East London northwards and westwards into Gauteng, Zimbabwe and Mozambique, with another population in central Namibia, through Caprivi to the Zimbabwean border.

The **Smooth dombeya** (*D. cymosa*) is another conspicuous, but more slender tree. Its leaves are much more pointed and not as thick and leathery as those of the Wild-pear dombeya. It occurs from East London, below the escarpment and north along the Lebombo Mountains.

The **Pink dombeya** (*D. burgessiae*) has very large, velvety, nearly round leaves (60–200 mm) with three lobes. Its distribution is similar to that of the Smooth dombeya, but it also occurs in central to northeastern Zimbabwe.

ML

Top: **Pink dombeyas** have striking pink flowers borne in fairly compact inflorescences. ***Bottom:*** They have big, hairy, soft leaves with conspicuous venation.

ML

In some areas **Wild-pear dombeyas** flower while leafless, in others the flowers and last year's leaves occur together.

The leaves of the **Wild-pear dombeya** are rounded, tough and hairy with a well-developed reticulum of veins on their under-surfaces.

Smooth dombeya flowers are sweet-scented. The white petals turn rusty brown as the fruits ripen.

Hanging inflorescences and leaves of a **Lowveld star-chestnut**.

HFG

BW

Left: **Bushveld tick-trees** typically have simple deeply lobed leaves. *Right:* The fruits are characteristic for the genus.

Bushveld tick-trees usually have startling silver-white trunks.

HFG

Bushveld tick-tree: view of the trunk showing the smooth striated bark.

Notes

- Dombeyas make showy garden shrubs and small trees.
- The fruit of the Lowveld star-chestnut needs to be handled with care, as inside the capsule there is a multitude of hairs that can cause great irritation.

The star-chestnuts (*Sterculia* spp.) are another group that are well represented regionally:

Perhaps the most common is the **Lowveld star-chestnut** (*S. murex*), which occurs on rocky sites in the Lebombo Mountains, extending westwards into Botswana, and just north into Zimbabwe and to the southern coast of Mozambique. This small tree has a swollen trunk and leaves that are soft, greyish-green above and buff and velvety below.

The **Bushveld tick-tree** (*S. africana*) is a squat multi-stemmed tree that occurs in hot dry areas, often bordering mopane bushveld. It is found in northern Namibia and along the Zambezi valley. The simple leaves are crowded near the twig ends, and the bark is silver or, sometimes, brownish.

Three colas (*Cola* spp.) occur in the region. All have simple glossy leaves with entire margins. The leaves are much longer than they are wide, with two pronounced swellings on the petiole: one at the leaf base and the other where the petiole is attached to the stem. Young leaves can be finely hairy. Colas usually occur in localised groves. The **Southern cola** (*Cola natalensis*) is the most widespread.

EvJ

GG

The leaves of a **Southern cola** have a double bump on the petiole (see arrows) and strap-shaped leaves.

Baobabs also belong to the hibiscus family. In Africa there is only one species of baobab (~6 spp. in Madagascar and 1sp. in Australia).

The **African baobab** (*Adansonia digitata*) is, arguably, the most conspicuous and widely known species of large tree in subtropical and tropical Africa. Its leaves (when present) are digitate and spirally arranged (200–300 mm long). The trunk can be enormous, while the branches are short and squat. The smooth pinkish-grey to coppery bark can be heavily folded. The flowers are waxy and white (up to 200 mm), while the fruits are extremely hard woody capsules (80–200 mm long) densely covered in short, velvety, yellowish hairs. African baobabs are important both to humans and to many animal species, and have, consequently, been widely dispersed. They occur in arid regions as well as in the bushveld, close to Iron Age sites. Despite their huge size they can be difficult to spot when in full leaf. This camouflage does not last long because they shed their leaves and flowers quickly. However, the fruits persist for much longer, sometimes as long as a year.

African baobabs may grow quite quickly: this lowveld specimen is just 6 years old. Claims that some trees are >1 000 years old are dubious.

Insets: EvJ

African baobabs lose their leaves in the dry winter months. Despite their size and unmistakable appearance they are well camouflaged when they are in full leaf during the wetter summer season. ***Inset left:*** The large, hard, woody capsule encloses a white pulp that surrounds many kidney-shaped seeds. This pulp was the original source of cream of tartar, used for baking. ***Inset right:*** The large showy flowers last just a few days.

Dwarf false-baobabs

Vitaceae, Pedaliaceae, Apocynaceae, & Crassulaceae

Namibian kobas bear large fleshy leaves during the wet season.

In the region there are four families with dwarf baobab-like trees, which all occur in arid regions. This means that the trees are:

- ✓ stout
- ✓ squat
- ✓ small
- ✓ generally leafless for most of the year

The Grape family (Vitaceae) includes three dwarf trees found in rocky habitats in the northwest of Namibia. One of these three can reach the size of a small tree, namely the **Namibian kobas** (*Cyphostemma currorii*). When leaves are present, these are large, compound and fleshy (>100 mm).

The Sesame family (Pedaliaceae) includes three small trees that occur in rocky habitats in northwestern Namibia. The two most common species are the **Herero sesame-bush** (*Sesamothamnus guerichii*) and the **Kaoko sesame-bush** (*S. benguellensis*). They all bear leaves only after rain and then for just a month or so. Sesame-bushes are spiny, so are easy to distinguish from other false-baobabs.

EvJ

Unlike the other sesame-bushes, which have white flowers, those of the **Herero sesame-bush** are distinctly yellow.

The **Kaoko sesame-bush** is also spinescent. It occurs most commonly on rocky, sand-covered ridges in northwestern Namibia.

In the Oleander family (Apocynaceae) there are two small baobab-like bushveld species: the **Namibian impala-lily** (*Adenium boehmianum*) occurs in northern Namibia, while the **Bushveld impala-lily** (*A. multiflorum*) occurs in the east from northern KwaZulu-Natal into Zimbabwe and Mozambique. Both species produce copious milky latex and have trumpet-shaped brightly coloured flowers that are highly conspicuous. The trees bear highly glossy leaves for a short period.

In the Crassula Family (Crassulaceae) there is one small baobab-like tree that occurs in the Karoo, usually on little hills or on rocky sites, namely the **Cape butter-tree** (*Tylecodon paniculatus*) or *Botterboom*. It has succulent leaves that last a short while after rain.

Namibian impala-lily flowers are trumpet-shaped and bright pink.

When protected from large herbivores, the **Bushveld impala-lily** produces a mass of spectacular flowers.

This **Bushveld impala-lily** has been sheltered from browsing animals and is therefore quite large.

Cape butter-trees grow in the winter-rainfall region and are therefore summer deciduous. They bear leaves during the wet winter months **(*left*)** and then lose them to conserve water during summer (***above***).

Fibre-bark Family

Thymelaeaceae ~900 spp. globally; ~10 spp. regionally, ~5. spp. of tree

EvJ

In full flower, **African pompom-trees** make extremely attractive horticultural subjects.
Inset left: Leaf detail showing the looping venation.
Inset right: The flowers occur in tight apical clusters.

The bark of a **Forest poison-olive** strips easily to make the stringy fibres that give this family its common name.

Notes

- Because the bark strips so easily into fibres, it has been used extensively to make string and rope, and is even plaited to tie down thatch.

Plants in this fairly large family typically:

- ✓ are woody, with bark that strips easily
- ✓ have leaves that are alternate, simple, entire and lack stipules
- ✓ are shrubs, although there are a few small to medium-sized trees

The following are widespread members of the family:

African pompom-tree (*Dais cotinifolia*) is usually small to medium-sized and is conspicuous when in flower. It occurs mostly at the edges of afromontane forest, on rocky outcrops from East London to the northern Drakensberg, and in the Chimanimani Mountains. The flowers, bluish-green leaves and neat rounded canopy are characteristic.

Forest poison-olives (*Peddiea africana*) are afromontane and coastal forest subcanopy shrubs that may attain the height of a small tree. The leaves, flowers and fruits are diagnostic.

Forest poison-olive flowers are green or cream, but sometimes pinkish. They may have reddish floral tubes.

RELATED SPECIES: *Passerina* spp. (gonnas) are also members of this family. Mostly single-stemmed, <3 m tall with tiny hard leaves (2–10 mm) that tend to lie flat on the twigs, they are fairly widespread in sandy soils along the coast and in some mountains and superficially resemble *Erica* spp.

Typical leaf arrangement of *Passerina* spp.

Meranti Family

Dipterocarpaceae

~500 spp. globally; 3 spp. regionally, all trees

This pan-tropical family of woody plants occurs mostly in southeast Asia. The following are key characteristics:

- ✓ all species are woody
- ✓ the bark is wrinkled in the bend where a big branch occurs
- ✓ leaves are simple, spirally arranged and have a distinctive tiny spot on the midrib, close to where the petiole meets the leaf blade

Monotes spp. occur in miombo bushveld: these small to medium-sized trees are found only in Zimbabwe and western Mozambique.

Among the most conspicuous, because of its pale yellowish-green foliage, is the **Pale-fruit monotes** (*Monotes glabra*), which usually occurs on sandy soils.

The other fairly common and widespread miombo bushveld species is the **Pink-fruit monotes** (*M. engleri*), which is distinguished from the Pale-fruit monotes by having darker green leaves with less of a tapering base and apex. The leaves are usually rounded and may be notched.

BW

Pale-fruit monotes: note the narrow leaf shape and the veins that loop at the margins.

HFG

Pale-fruit monotes have ephemeral stipules and pale green leaves.

BW

Pale-fruit monotes flower and leaf.

TC (incl. inset)

Pink-fruit monotes have characteristic roundish leaves that separate this species from the Pale-fruit monotes. ***Inset:*** The Pink-fruit monotes derives its name from the colour of its fruits.

Pink-fruit monotes bark is wrinkled in the bends where big branches occur.

TC

Spekboom Family

Didiereaceae

12 spp. globally; 2 spp. regionally, both trees

A lone **African spekboom** tree on a rocky cliff in the Kruger National Park.

African spekbooms have opposite, roundish, succulent leaves, each with a tiny mucro at the apex.

Notes

- African spekbooms are susceptible to overbrowsing by domestic livestock but not by large African mammals such as elephant and kudu. Research has demonstrated that this has to do with the way the plant grows. If browsed top-down, the plant survives well because the lowest branches can break off and take root. However, browsing from the bottom up, which is what goats (the main culprits) and cattle do, severely damages this tree's regenerative capacity.
- The leaves of spekboom are edible. Interestingly, they are sweet in the morning and sour in the late afternoon. This is because of the way they photosynthesise.

The two species in this family are both small trees, and are easy to identify. They have the following characteristics:

- ✓ succulent stems
- ✓ succulent leaves

The **African spekboom** (*Portulacaria afra*) occurs commonly in the eastern Karoo and was a major component of the Addo bushveld inland of Port Elizabeth, a vegetation type that has become more rare because it is overgrazed by domestic livestock. This tree also occurs scattered through rocky bushveld as far north as the Lebombo Mountains. The leaves are distinctive, opposite, roundish, and up to 30 mm long.

The ummistakable **Namaqua porkbush** (*Ceraria namaquensis*) has silvery bark and small deciduous leaves that occur in clusters on tiny dwarf branches.

AJ

A small branch of a **Namaqua porkbush** in full leaf. ***Inset:*** The leaves are produced on dwarf shoots that resemble blackish bumps.

Namaqua porkbushes have whitish succulent stems. Tiny succulent leaves are produced on small blackish bumps.

Assegai Family

Curtisiaceae

2 spp. globally, endemic to Africa, both trees

This family includes two genera, each with one species. Members of the family have:

- ✓ opposite leaves
- ✓ tiny yellowish-green flowers borne in terminal clusters
- ✓ small and thinly fleshy fruits (~10 mm long)

The genus *Curtisia* is monospecific, that is, it comprises just one genus, which is uncommon. The characteristics of the species are illustrated and described in the captions to the photographs.

African assegai (*Curtisia dentata*) is a readily identifiable, medium to large tree, usually found in afromontane forest and occasionally in rocky areas, from Cape Town to the Soutpansberg and in the Zimbabwean eastern highlands to Mount Gorongoza.

African assegai trees coppice easily and frequently, and can be managed to produce a good supply of straight poles, laths and spear shafts.

An **African assegai** cannot be mistaken for any other tree in the region. The new shoots are pinkish and softly hairy. Note also the distinctly opposite leaves.

Flower buds are borne in terminal bunches.

Note the urn-shaped form of the petiole base (see arrow), which is a feature of the species.

Leaf upper-surface showing U-shaped marginal serrations and the typical petiole base from which the leaves arise.

Leaf under-surface showing the distinctive venation: the veins loop just before the margin, but tiny veins run to the serrations.

Notes

- These trees produce very straight, thin, upright branches that can be harvested to make assegai shafts, hence the common name. (Another common name for the species is the Cape lancewood.)

Milkwood Family

Sapotaceae

~800 spp. globally; ~22 spp. regionally, all trees

The natural habitat of **White milkwoods** is coastal bush, dry forest or bush clumps in the bushveld. Old trees usually have a gnarled appearance. ***Inset:*** Leaves have a translucent yellow halo. The veins, even the tiniest ones, are translucent when held against the light.

The milkwood family is one of the most easily recognisable regionally. The following are distinctive features:

- ✓ milky latex – particularly easy to see on fresh young twigs when a leaf is removed
- ✓ leaves are simple, entire and alternate, dark green and generally more glossy above than below
- ✓ leaves lack a large leaf scar (which distinguishes this family from the figs)
- ✓ young growth is often rusty or brownish
- ✓ all have fleshy fruits and glossy seeds (in shades of brown)

White milkwoods (*Sideroxylon inerme*) are among the most widespread and easily recognised small to medium-sized (rarely large) trees in the family. They have dense canopies and gnarled branches. The elliptic leaves are dull below and a translucent rim surrounds the leaf. These trees occur along, or close to, the coast from Cape Town almost to Beira, often in thickets. From KwaZulu-Natal northwards the species can occur further inland, often on termitaria in bushveld and on riparian fringes.

Red-milkwoods are generally medium-sized trees with dense canopies, and leaves that are *not* strongly clustered. The following are some common examples:

Coast red-milkwoods (*Mimusops caffra*) are dune forest specialists found from East London to Beira and can be locally common. A characteristic feature is that the leaves (25–50 mm long) are stiff and leathery, silvery to pale bronze below, with a bluntish apex, and a strongly rolled-under margin.

Bushveld red-milkwoods (*M. obovata*) occur in low-altitude forest from north of East London to the Lebombo Mountains. They can also be found in bushveld or in rocky habitats. The leaves are thinly leathery, elliptic (20–60 mm), with a slightly rolled-under margin.

EvJ

Typical fruit of the **Coast red-milkwood.** Note the persistent style, which looks like a tiny black thread. The leaves are tough with a rounded apex and rolled margins.

Bushveld red-milkwood fruits **(*above*)** have more elongated tips than those of the Coast red-milkwood. The flower's form is typical of the genus. The leaves **(*left*)** are more elliptic and paler below than those of the Coast red-milkwood.

The **Moepel red-milkwood** (*M. zeyheri*) has leaves with longish petioles – up to 30 mm compared with <10 mm for the previous two species. These trees are widespread in bushveld and grow at wettish sites, including on rocky outcrops and in riparian areas. They occur at lower altitudes from the east coast to Mahikeng and northwards to the Zambezi.

Milkplums (*Englerophytum* spp.) are small to medium-sized trees and are easily identified by their striking bicoloured leaves, which tend to be clustered on the twig ends. The following are some common examples:

The unmistakable **Stamvrug milkplum** (*E. magalismontanum*) has dense silver to golden-brown, even bronze, hairs on its leaf under-surfaces. The leaf upper-surface has blue-green bloom that is easily wiped off. The leaves tend to hang and have a rounded apex. These small to medium-sized trees occur in rocky areas, often in small groves, from northern KwaZulu-Natal westwards to Mahikeng and northwards to the Limpopo. They are also found in the eastern parts of Zimbabwe.

The **Silver-leaved milkplum** (*E. natalense*) is a small to medium-sized tree found in the forest subcanopy, or in wooded ravines. It occurs from East London northwards and along the Lebombo Mountains, as well as in the eastern highlands of Zimbabwe. The leaves can be held distinctly horizontally, as can the branches. Young leaves are covered in dark brown hairs. Older leaves are silvery below with a tapering apex.

JB

EvJ

Moepel red-milkwoods have yellowish flowers held on long hairy stalks. ***Inset:*** The fruits are more spherical than those of the other red-milkwoods.

EvJ

Leaves that are blue-green above and golden-brown below are diagnostic of the **Stamvrug milkplum,** as is the boat-shaped leaf form.

EvJ

A **Stamvrug milkplum** in full fruit. Note that the fruit is borne on old wood – hence this tree's common name, which means 'stem fruit' in Afrikaans.

Silver-leaved milkplums have silver-backed leaves. Note that this leaf was twisted to show the under-surface and is exuding milky latex at the break.

Notes

- The fruits of all species in this family are edible. Many are not especially palatable, although those of the milkplums are particularly delicious. However, great caution must be exercised in determining the species correctly, as some similar-looking species in other families bear extremely toxic fruits. One example is Bushman's poison-bush (*Acokanthera oppositifolia*).
- Stamvrug milkplum fruits are delicious and are highly sought-after.

There are three fairly widespread species of milkberry, ranging in size from small to large.

Zulu milkberries (*Manilkara concolor*) are generally small trees that occur in low-altitude forest, fairly close to the coast, from Port St Johns to Beira. The leaves tend to be crowded apically (25–70 mm) and have a yellowish midrib that is slightly ridged above and prominent below. The apex is rounded and often notched.

Forest milkberries (*M. discolor*) generally grow in low-altitude dry forest from Port St Johns to north of Beira. The dark grey bark is longitudinally fissured and the trunks of large trees are a little fluted. Young shoots have brownish hairs. The leaves are clustered on the twig apices. Mature leaves are bluish-green above, silvery with densely packed hairs below, and have a rounded apex.

Lowveld milkberries (*M. mochisia*) range in size from spreading shrubs to medium-sized trees and are found in hot dry bushveld, often on termite mounds. They occur from northern KwaZulu-Natal northwards to southern Zimbabwe and in the Zambezi valley, with an outlier population along the Cunene River. The leaves are clustered on short stubby branches that give the twigs a knobbly effect. The leaves are smallish (15–50 mm), light green above, pale brown and hairy below, and have a rounded and notched apex.

TL

A **Zulu milkberry** with plump round fruits and typical apically clustered leaves. Note the notched apex.

TW

Upper-surface of a **Zulu milkberry** leaf showing the grooved midrib and fairly inconspicuous side veins. The leaf apex can be spout-like.

Forest milkberry showing the whitish leaf under-surfaces and fine herringbone venation. The leaves tend to be crowded towards the twig ends.

TC

Lowveld milkberry fruits are smallish. Note that the leaves in this specimen are smaller than usual because it is growing in a harsh environment.

Lowveld milkberries can be identified by their growth form: blunt-tipped leaves occur in apical rosettes on stiff, nearly horizontal twigs.

The medium-sized **Forest bush-milkwood** (*Vitellariopsis marginata*) grows in low-altitude forest, in scrub, in ravines, and along drainage lines from East London northwards through Swaziland and almost to Beira. The light brown bark exfoliolates in small stringy strips. The branching pattern is characteristic, with short upright twigs carrying a rosette of leaves apically. Young leaves are bright red. The leaves are distinctly quilted with a rounded to broadly tapering apex and a pale yellow midrib.

African milk-pears (*Inhambanella henriquesii*) are large trees found in coastal forest from north of Durban to Maputo, and on the Chimanimani Mountains. New leaves are a bright copper red that makes the whole tree conspicuous. The mature leaves are broadly elliptic (50–170 mm long), pleated, with long petioles (20–45 mm) and a rounded apex that may bend backwards. They have translucent, sometimes wavy, margins.

The **Fluted forest-milkwood** (*Chrysophyllum viridifolium*) is a large tree found in coastal forest. The species is named for its fluted trunk. These trees occur from north of East London to southern Maputo and in the Chimanimani Mountains. The leaves have many closely spaced lateral veins (<2 mm apart) that end in a conspicuous marginal vein.

The lateral veins in the leaves of a **Fluted forest-milkwood** end just short of the margin, where they join a vein that runs round the edge of the leaf.

Fluted forest-milkwoods can be huge trees. Their trunks are characteristically fluted.

HFG

AS, JB (inset)

Terminal leaf rosette of a **Forest bush-milkwood.** The lateral veins are fairly conspicuous. ***Inset:*** The flower buds are borne on long recurved stalks and the leaves on pale maroon-brown petiole bases.

HFG

The mature leaves of the **African milk-pear** are pale green and shiny above.

African milk-pears are readily distinguished by the striking young red leaves as well as the long petioles.

Ebony Family

Ebenaceae

~550 spp. globally; ~35 spp. regionally, ~30 spp. of tree

Small-leaved guarri in full fruit. The purplish-black fruits are ripe. Note the tiny leaves with strongly undulating margins.

BW

The Zimbabwean form of **Blue guarri** has hairy, rust-coloured young foliage.

Blue guarris have highly variable leaves, depending on the region in which they occur. These are the leaves of the central bushveld form.

A **Magic guarri** in full fruit – some green and some ripe. Note the typical leaf shape, venation and colour.

Vegetatively this family of evergreens is not very distinctive, although it is characterised by having simple entire leaves that lack stipules, and by a persistent calyx on the fruit. However, the guarris (~12 species) and two other regional genera, the jackal-berries and star-apples (~26 species), are more easily characterised. They have leaves that:

- ✓ generally are narrowly elliptic
- ✓ tend to be hard and leathery
- ✓ have margins that often undulate
- ✓ are generally opposite to subopposite
- ✓ are often covered with fine rust-coloured hairs when young

Guarris are usually multi-stemmed bushes or small trees. The following are some more common species:

The **Small-leaved guarri** (*Euclea undulata*) occurs widely in the region but is absent from the West Coast, Kalahari, grassland areas and much of Zimbabwe and Mozambique. This small neat tree or bush is found mostly on open rocky sites, occasionally forming thickets. Leaves are generally small (20–50 mm), broadly elliptic (but sometimes quite narrow), with very wavy margins. Sometimes they are tinged rusty brown below. A diagnostic feature is that young growth is covered with minute brown granules.

Blue guarris (*E. crispa*) are similar to Small-leaved guarris, but the leaves tend to be longer and narrower, with a rounded apex and slightly wavy margins. They are generally bluish-green and pliable, but vary considerably across their range. These trees occur from about Cape Agulhas northwards through the Karoo and bushveld to Limpopo, with an outlier population in northern to central Zimbabwe.

Magic guarris (*E. divinorum*) are small multi-stemmed trees or shrubs that occur in bushveld, commonly on seasonally waterlogged sites where they grow in groves. They are found through KwaZulu-Natal into Zimbabwe and westwards into Caprivi. The elliptic leaves (35–80 mm) are stiff, leathery and often finely wrinkled. Their veins are translucent, and the margins are wavy.

Hairy guarris (*E. natalensis*) have among the most highly variable leaf morphology of any tree. The leaves are almost round in individuals on the northern KwaZulu-Natal coast, but narrowly elliptic on trees at higher altitudes in the North West province. Typically, they are broadest in the apical third and have a fairly rounded apex. Leaf size varies (40–140 mm, but usually ~70 mm). Young leaves are densely covered in rust-coloured hairs and even mature leaves may have a few hairs on the under-surface. This species occurs on rocky outcrops and in bushveld, riparian areas and dry forest. It is found from the Western Cape eastwards and northwards to the North West province, and on the Chimanimani Mountains.

The **Dune guarri** (*E. racemosa*) is easily identified by its small round-tipped leaves, which have tightly rolled margins (20–50 mm). It has a dense canopy and often forms impenetrable thickets. It is restricted to coastal sands from the Orange River mouth southwards and westwards to Port Elizabeth. Another distinctive guarri is the **Black-ebony guarri** (*E. pseudebenus*) – a small tree with drooping branches that grows along drainage lines and in riparian areas from the Cunene River southwards to Namaqualand.

The leaves of the **Hairy guarri** are variable, but these are the typical form: the outer third of the leaf is broadest, the margins are wavy and the veins are yellowish. Only young leaves are conspicuously hairy.

Mature **Black-ebony guarris** have weeping branches that resemble those of a willow. They are riparian specialists in arid areas in the western parts of southern Africa.

EvJ

Dune guarri with typical rounded, stiff, upright leaves and tightly rolled margins. The fruits turn black when ripe.

Dune guarris have small creamy white flowers.

Stiff tough leaves, held at right angles to the twigs, separate the **Black-ebony guarri** from the willows, which have hanging, soft and pliable leaves.

Notes

- The wood of most guarris is hard, and the heartwood almost black. Most species do not have palatable leaves, so the species may proliferate where the habitat has been degraded by overgrazing.
- Generally the leaves have a 'guarri' look: they are stiff, tough and smallish with squiggly yellowish lateral veins.
- In guarri species male and female flowers occur on separate trees.

EvJ

Left: **Ebony jackal-berries** are large lowveld trees with drooping foliage and blackish bark. They often grow along rivers. *Right:* Twig with a few drooping leaves and ripening fruits. Note the persistent calyx lobes where a fruit has been plucked (see arrow).

Another important genus in the ebony family is *Diospyros*, which includes the jackal-berries, bladder-nuts and star-apples. They range in size from bushes to large trees, but all have simple alternate leaves that are broadly elliptic and mostly pliable. The calyx is conspicuous on the fruits of these species and is five lobed in the star-apples, an envelope in the bladder-nuts, and cup-shaped in the jackal-berries.

Ebony jackal-berries (*D. mespiliformis*) can be imposing trees. They are medium to large with a dense rounded canopy and blackish bark. They are scattered through low- to medium-altitude bushveld, often on termitaria or in riparian areas, and are found from northern KwaZulu-Natal through Limpopo and Mozambique to Zimbabwe, and westwards to the Kaokoveld in northwestern Namibia. The oblong to elliptic leaves (45–100 mm long) are glossy green above, paler below. They start to turn yellow in autumn and new leaves appear as the old leaves fall. On occasion old leaves fall and young leaves take a few days or weeks to grow, so these generally evergreen trees can be briefly deciduous. The fruits taste much like persimmons.

Acorn jackal-berries (*D. natalensis*) are small trees found in dune and coastal forest, and are confined to the coastal strip from East London to north of Beira. They bear small, neat, roundish leaves (15–30 mm) on very slender twigs.

CV

An **Acorn jackal-berry** in full fruit. Note the cup-shaped calyx at the base of the fruit. This species gets its common name from the fact that the fruits look rather like tiny acorns.

CV

Acorn jackal-berries have neat roundish leaves on very slightly zigzagging twigs.

Crocodile-bark jackal-berries (*D. quiloensis*) have similar fruits to those of the Acorn jackal-berry but bigger leaves (40–60 mm) that are borne on short knobbly branches. They are restricted to the Zambezi valley and Chimanimani Mountain region, often in mopane bushveld.

Bluebush star-apples (*D. lycioides*) occur in bushveld throughout much of the region, but are absent from the central Kalahari and Mozambique, as well as from desert and fynbos vegetation. They rarely grow into small trees, more frequently occurring as conspicuous, rounded, tall bushes. The leaves (15–70 mm) tend to be crowded on the twig apices and are broadest in the apical third. They are dull green, have a rounded apex and tapering base and, when young, are covered with silky hairs. The fruits are almost spherical with five persistent calyx lobes that bend strongly backwards. There are a number of similar star-apples, so identification can be tricky.

Sand star-apples (*Diospyros loureiriana*) are small trees with fairly large leaves (30–100 mm) that have a broadly tapering apex and a rounded base. They occur in bushveld and thicket on sandy soils in northeastern South Africa, eastern Zimbabwe and southern Mozambique. Their range overlaps marginally with the similar Bluebush star-apple.

Bladder-nut species are widespread and locally common in forest, scrub and rocky environments:

The **Forest bladder-nut** (*D. whyteana*) occurs in forests below the coastal mountain ranges from the Cape Peninsula to Port Elizabeth, as well as more widely in forest environments up to the Limpopo River and in central and eastern Zimbabwe. This is a small tree with very glossy leaves (25–40 mm), the margins of which are fringed with ginger hairs. Hairs also occur on the leaf under-surfaces.

BW

Crocodile-bark jackal-berries get their common name from their bark, which resembles the scales of a crocodile.

The leaves of the **Bluebush star apple** have conspicuous veins and a quilted upper-surface. The fruits are soft and fleshy. ***Inset:*** This specimen has smaller, hairier leaves and fruits and the calyx lobes are reflexed. This is a widespread species and there is some degree of variation across its range.

The new leaves of a **Forest bladder-nut** are much more conspicuously hairy than older leaves. ***Inset:*** The species is identified by the bladder-like calyx lobes enveloping the fruit. The fruit is not a nut, despite the common name.

EW

A **Sand star-apple** is easily identified by the large calyx lobes that almost cover the fruit.

False-assegai Family

Maesaceae

1 sp. globally, endemic to the region, a tree

AS

A typical **False-assegai** in grassland habitat.

The classification of the family is disputed. The genus *Maesa*, which includes many species, is placed in its own family. The same group also contains the heaths (Ericaceae). Key characteristics of Maesaceae are as follows:

- ✓ leaves are alternate and serrate
- ✓ flowers are often galled and are then persistent

False-assegai (*Maesa lanceolata*) is a widespread, small, straggling tree occurring on rocky outcrops, afromontane forest edges and along rivers from Port St Johns to the Soutpansberg, and in central and eastern Zimbabwe. The simple, alternate, serrate leaves can be glossy above and are brownish and hairy with prominent veins below.

AS (both)

The fruits are small and whitish. ***Inset:*** The leaves are distinctive, slightly quilted and have evenly serrate margins. The tips of the serrations are rounded like the teeth of a blunt saw.

Notes

- False-assegais survive fires quite well and may be seen where grassland and bushveld, or forest and grassland, border each other, particularly from central KwaZulu-Natal northwards. These small, shrubby, often untidy trees are conspicuous and widespread.

AS

The flowers of a **False-assegai** are tiny and cream-coloured and may be produced *en masse*.

Myrsine Family

Myrsinaceae ~1 000 spp. globally; 5 spp. regionally, 1 spp. of tree

The trunks are often very straight and – in older trees – reasonably unbranched, with a cylindrical canopy. They tend to grow together and characteristically have:

- ✓ smoothish bark
- ✓ large warty protuberances (called pustules) that are ~10 mm in diameter
- ✓ conspicuous leaf scars on the twigs

Within our region this family includes only one tree, the **Large cape-beech** (*Rapanea melanophleos*), or *Boekenhout* in Afrikaans. It can be quite large and has been known to reach a height of 20 m. This is a widespread forest subcanopy, forest edge and riparian species. It can be locally common and is easily identified by the leathery, matt, dark green leaves, which have maroon-purplish petioles.

The leaves have many slightly squiggly lateral veins. However, the venation is not easily visible. The leaves tend to be clumped apically and the bare twigs are quite rough.

Inspection of the twigs reveals conspicuous, distinctive scars (resembling bumps) where leaves have fallen.

The **Large Cape-beech** typically produces copious tiny fruits towards the tips of the twigs. They are blackish-purple when ripe.

The bark of the **Large cape-beech** is diagnostic: it is greyish and fairly smooth, except for vertical rows of wart-like structures called pustules.

Notes

- A similar species, the Small cape-beech (*Rapanea gilliana*), occurs in forest and dunes along the Eastern Cape coast. It may occasionally attain the height of a small tree.
- The timber of the Large cape-beech is finely grained and is still sometimes used in furniture-making.

Heath Family

Ericaceae

>1 000 spp. globally; ~700 spp. regionally, ~8 spp. of tree

RB

Though it has tiny, bell-shaped, erica-like flowers, the **African blueberry** has broad alternate leaves, quite unlike those of the *Erica* spp.

Cape tree-ericas die from the bottom up, which ensures that they burn quickly and completely in a fire. They regenerate mostly from seeds.

The flowers of the **Water tree-erica** resemble tiny bells. Like most ericas this species flowers prolifically.

The leaves of the **Water tree-erica** are quite tightly rolled and are white below. They occur in whorls.

Notes

- The ripe fruits of the African blueberry are edible and make good jam.
- Scottish heathers are closely related to our *Erica* species.
- When not in flower ericas can be confused with species in other families that also have tiny leaves. However, these other species often differ in that the tiny leaves are not tightly rolled and/or arranged in whorls.

In southern Africa, the heath family includes two genera: one has a single species, the African blueberry, which is rare; the other is the very large genus *Erica*, which has ~700 species. This family is easily recognised by the following features, although the African blueberry's leaves differ:

- ✓ tiny bell-shaped or small tubular flowers
- ✓ tiny leaves (1–10 mm long)
- ✓ tightly rolled leaf margins (except in the African blueberry)
- ✓ leaves that are mostly whorled
- ✓ very finely branched twigs

The **African blueberry** (*Vaccinium exul*) is a small, rarely medium-sized, tree that occurs in mountainous areas from Swaziland to the Soutpansberg. It has bell-shaped flowers and rounded, fleshy red fruits (~7 mm diameter) that turn black when ripe.

All *Erica* species are woody and few grow to >2 m. They generally occur at higher altitudes in rocky areas in grassland, or mixed with other similar-sized shrubs. These species are characteristic of African heathlands, which are known locally as fynbos. They often have very showy flowers, which range from tiny bells to large tubes (20-30 mm long). Although they rarely grow into small trees, three tree-like species include the **Cape tree-erica** (*E. tristis*), found in fynbos and rocky areas, the **Water tree-erica** (*E. caffra*), which occurs in riparian situations and on forest edges (extending from the Cape to the KwaZulu-Natal/Lesotho Drakensberg), and the **Petrolbush erica** (*E. hexandra*) of eastern Zimbabwe.

BW

The flowers of the **Petrolbush erica** are a deep pink.

White-pear Family

Icacinaceae ~150 spp. globally; 5 spp. regionally, 3 spp. of tree

The Large white-pear is the only big tree species in the family regionally. Family characteristics include the following:

- ✓ simple alternate leaves
- ✓ leaves glossy above and dull below
- ✓ leaves variable in size (20–30 or 45–100 mm)

Large white-pears (*Apodytes dimidiata*) are widespread from Cape Town to the Limpopo River and westwards to Mahikeng. They also occur in eastern and central Zimbabwe. Although primarily a forest species, this tree can be found in a wide range of moist habitats, but is absent from arid bushveld.

The family also includes a more scrambling species that occasionally attains the height of a small tree, namely the **Lemon-thorn cassinopsis** (*Cassinopsis ilicifolia*). It has green branches that zigzag noticeably, and opposite leaves with occasional straight spines. The margins may be entire or serrate.

The **Lemon-thorn cassinopsis** has glossy opposite leaves with serrate margins, occasional spines and tiny flowers. ***Inset:*** The small fruits are fleshy and orange when ripe.

Large white-pear fruits are diagnostic. They comprise a black seed surrounded by a bright red fleshy cap called an aril.

Large white-pears typically have smooth greyish bark and similar lichen patterns throughout the region.

The under-surface of a **Large white-pear** leaf showing the very slightly rolled margins.

A typical leaf of the **Large white-pear** showing the mid-vein, which ends just before the apex. Note the yellowish margins and the red to maroon petiole.

Notes

- Along the coast and at low altitudes Large white-pear leaves tend to be big and hairless. At high altitudes the leaves are far smaller and may be a little hairy, particularly on the under-surfaces. High-altitude plants tend to be compact and twiggy, quite different from those growing at lower altitudes.

Coffee Family

Rubiaceae

~13 000 spp. globally; ~240 spp. regionally, ~100 spp. of tree

A young hairy fruit showing the calyx lobes that are characteristic of a **Gummy gardenia**. *Inset:* Small drops of resin oozing from the twig confirm the identity of this species. Interpetiolar stipules can be seen at the left of the twig.

This is the second-largest family in the region and species are easily recognised by:

- ✓ simple, opposite (occasionally whorled) leaves that have interpetiolar stipules, or a scar once the stipules have fallen
- ✓ leaves with an entire margin
- ✓ pockets often found in the axils of the veins on the leaf under-surface

In southern Africa, most species in this family are shrubs or small trees, with a few notable exceptions. In some genera the species can be quite difficult to differentiate, but in others they are readily identifiable.

Gardenias, rothmannias and loquats are a group of shrubs and small trees that all have quite large, sweetly scented white or pale flowers (>10 mm diameter), as well as fairly large, woody, persistent fruits.

There are 7 species of *Gardenia*, all with white to yellow tubular flowers (>30 mm in diameter), ovoid fruits (>15 mm long) and rigid three-whorled leaves. These species are usually multiple-stemmed bushes and small trees. The four most widespread all occur in thicket, bushveld, riparian bush or dry forest:

Gummy gardenias (*G. resiniflua*) occur in northern Limpopo and throughout much of Zimbabwe, but are absent in the east. The leaves are velvety when young, but rough above and velvety below when mature.

Powder-bark gardenias (*G. ternifolia*) are found from the Okavango eastwards through much of northern, eastern and central Zimbabwe, and in northeastern Limpopo. The bark is smooth, powdery and rubs off. It also peels off in roundish pieces.

Forest gardenias (*G. thunbergia*) occur from Knysna to northern KwaZulu-Natal. The persistent fruits (~70–35 mm) are greyish and fairly smooth, with raised whitish spots.

DP

The flowers of the **Powder-bark gardenia** turn pale yellow with age, hence its alternate name – the Yellow gardenia.

The whorled leaf arrangement and clasping stipules of a **Forest gardenia**.

Left: A thrip nymph and other tiny in-vertebrates in the hairy pocket on the under-surface of a **Forest gardenia** leaf. ***Right:*** Like all gardenias, they bear whorled leaves on hard, stubby, often pale branches. The pockets in the leaf's under-surface appear as bumps from above.

Forest gardenias can carry masses of their characteristic hard fruits. The fruits persist on the tree for many months.

Bushveld gardenias (*G. vokensii*) are the most widespread *Gardenia* species. They occur in KwaZulu-Natal and as far west as Mahikeng in North West province. Their range also extends into southern Mozambique, Zimbabwe, northern Botswana and Kaokoland in Namibia. Fruits are ovoid, almost round, ribbed, grey-green and covered with wart-like greyish lenticels.

Rothmannia spp. occur in southern Africa in forest, on forest edges or in wooded areas transitional to forest. The **Stately rothmannia** (*R. capensis*) is a forest species in the south, but can be found in forest-like bushveld vegetation in the west. It is 'replaced' by the Woodland rothmannia (*R. fischeri*), not pictured here, further to the north, but there is some overlap in their distribution on the Lembobo Mountains. The drooping leaves and bigger flowers of the Woodland rothmannia tend to distinguish the two species. Both are attractive in flower and have conspicuous persistent fruits and glossy dark green foliage.

The **September-bells rothmannia** (*R. globosa*) is usually a bush or small tree by comparison with the medium-sized trees discussed above. It has smaller flowers, and is distinguished by the reddish colour of the petioles, leaf midrib and lateral veins. This species occurs along forest edges and in wetter coastal bushveld from north of Port St Johns to northern KwaZulu-Natal. It also occurs through central Swaziland and into eastern Mpumalanga and Limpopo, as far as the Zimbabwean border.

The leaves of the **September-bells rothmannia** have a clasping interpetiolar petiole (see arrow) and diagnostic reddish midrib.

The fruits of the **Bushveld gardenia** are persistent and characteristically ribbed. ***Inset:*** This species has smoothish mottled bark.

EvJ

The flowers of **Stately rothmannias** are large open bells with speckling in the throat. ***Inset:*** There are conspicuous pockets in the leaf under-surface.

EvJ

September-bells rothmannias have bell-shaped flowers. In good years these trees may be nearly covered in sweet-smelling blossoms. ***Inset:*** The fruits are green, turning black with age, and have a persistent calyx.

EvJ

Bushveld spiny-gardenias have tubular flowers with pink-backed petals. The leaves are clustered on stubby branches. These branches may resemble spines.

EvJ

Bushveld spiny-gardenia twig architecture is opposite and then opposite again, making this an untidy tree. Note the spines.

Whipstick false-loquats have shorter floral tubes than those of the Sandforest false-loquat. The leaf bases are more equal and the venation more conspicuous. ***Inset:*** Note the long, attenuated interpetiolar stipule.

Notes

- Many gardenias make good garden subjects because their glossy dark green leaves, dense canopies, flowers and often persistent fruits make them very attractive.
- Bushveld spiny-gardenias make good hedges for small gardens.

Bushveld spiny-gardenias (*Hyperacanthus amoenus*) are small, straggling, very spiny trees with leaves that are crowded on dwarf branches. They occur from Knysna to the Lebombo Mountains, usually in dry forest, among rocks or along drainage lines.

The following are two of the three species of false-loquat, all of which are medium-sized or small trees:

Sandforest false-loquats (*Oxyanthus latifolius*) occur in sandforest from northern KwaZulu-Natal to Beira in Mozambique. They are distinguished by having large, asymmetric (50–180 mm), glossy dark green leaves and flowers with long tubes.

Whipstick false-loquats (*O. speciosus*) are small trees found in the forest subcanopy. They have distinctly horizontal branches and glossy dark green leaves (70–250 mm) and occur from Port St Johns up the coast to the Lebombo Mountains as far as the Limpopo River, as well as in the eastern highlands of Zimbabwe.

GN

Sandforest false-loquats have broad soft leaves with an unequal lobed base. Tiny white petals are borne on a long floral tube.

Whipstick false-loquat trees tend to have a slightly twisted trunk. The branches come off at 60–90 degrees. ***Inset:*** Fruits are usually borne in small bunches – these are immature.

The family includes the genus *Bronadia*, which has just one species regionally – the **African matumi** (*B. salicina*). This tree is found mostly along perennial rivers, sometimes in groves, from northern KwaZulu-Natal to the Zambezi, with an outlier population on the Limpopo west of Musina. The leaves (80–250 mm) are usually 3–4-whorled, elliptic, dark shiny green and more or less upright. (Although African quinine-trees are similar, they do not occur in this habitat, and have milky latex and much paler leaves that droop. See p. 156.)

The following three genera each comprise just one tree species:

Bride's-bush tarenna (*Tarenna pavettoides*) is a small to medium-sized tree found from Port St Johns to Swaziland and in the eastern highlands of Zimbabwe. It occurs in forest understorey and in swamp forest. The twigs are green to dark brown and four-angled, while the leaves (50–150 mm) are thinly textured and bright green. Small pockets are sometimes present on the leaves.

African wild-pomegranates (*Burchellia bubalina*) are widespread from Betty's Bay to the Lebombo Mountains as forest understorey shrubs or small trees. They grow on forest margins, on rocky outcrops and in riparian bush. They are easily identified by their showy scarlet to orange flowers and persistent fruits, which have soft, horn-like calyx lobes.

Magnificent-flame bushes (*Alberta magna*) are medium-sized and grow mainly on sandstone substrates in rocky areas, along forest edges and even in riparian bush. Because of the red to crimson flowers and, later, the winged red to crimson fruits, these trees are spectacular garden subjects.

African matumis are riparian specialists in the lowveld. ***Top inset:*** A leaf detail showing the many lateral veins and yellowish midrib. ***Bottom inset:*** The flowerheads are pendent, marble-sized, softly spiky spheres that look a bit like miniature medieval maces.

HFG (both)

The flowers of a **Bride's-bush tarenna** have large anthers. ***Inset:*** The leaves are large and softly textured with looping veins and a quilted upper-surface. Note the elongate drip-tip.

African wild-pomegranate flower. The leaves of this species have a quilted upper-surface.

Magnificent-flame bushes are aptly named because they have crimson flowers (shown on the left) that are followed by red-winged fruits (shown right).

JB

Velvet wild-medlar leaf under-surfaces and typical fruits. The fruits have a distinct circular scar (see arrow).

Kalahari wild-medlars typically have large leaves and tiny flowers and fruits.

BW

African false-medlar flowers have reflexed petals and upward-pointing pistils.

Notes

- All the medlars have edible fruits that are quite tasty. Generally they are rather untidy shrubs.

There are 11 species of wild-medlar of which two are dealt with here, as well as one false-medlar and one of the three pendent-medlars:

Velvet wild-medlars (*Vangueria infausta*) are the most widespread, occurring in bushveld from Port St Johns northwards and westwards to Kimberley. They also extend into Zimbabwe, northern Botswana and Namibia. These trees often grow in rocky areas, in sandy soils and among coastal scrub. The leaves are broadly elliptic and yellowish-brown (40–250 mm) and the fruits have a distinct circular scar left by the sometimes asymmetric calyx.

A small, weak tree, the **Kalahari wild-medlar** (*Vangueria cyanescens*) occurs from southern KwaZulu-Natal into Mpumalanga and Limpopo, on the border of Zimbabwe and Botswana, into Caprivi and westwards to Kaokoland. It grows best on sandy substrates in bushveld-like communities, and has thin, leathery, generally hairless leaves (80–150 mm).

The **African false-medlar** (*Vangueriopsis lanciflora*) is similar to the Velvet wild-medlar, but the leaves are dark and hairless above and markedly paler below, with woolly hairs. Those of the Velvet wild-medlar are mostly pale green and are hairy on both surfaces. African false-medlars occur from Owambo in Namibia eastwards to the border of Mozambique, in sandy bushveld, often on rocky sites.

There are three species of pendent-medlar in the region. They are so-named for their hanging fruits, which characteristically occur on slender stalks.

The **Smooth pendent-medlar** (*Lagynias lasiantha*) is a good example. This is a scrambling shrub or small weak tree found in coastal thicket and on forest edges from southern KwaZulu-Natal to southern Mozambique . This species is distinguished by its glossy green leaves, which are pale bluish-green below.

HFG

Smooth pendent-medlar fruits and typical bluish leaf under-surfaces.

Canthium is a big genus with ~15 species regionally. The following are three of the largest, most widespread and common species:

Velvety turkey-berries (*C. gilfillanii*) occur in rocky areas and in bushveld and are largely confined to the Limpopo and North West provinces. The leaves (25–50 mm) are thinly textured and velvety on both surfaces.

Criss-cross turkey-berries (*C. inerme*) are widespread, common, small to medium-sized trees found in coastal scrub and forest from Cape Town to the Lebombo Mountains, and in the eastern highlands of Zimbabwe. The leaves (25–90 mm) are hairless, glossy above and matt below, and the branchlets often have spine-tipped twigs that may be quite stout. The fruits tend to be two-lobed, about the size of goat droppings (the plant's Afrikaans name is *Bokdrol*), and can persist for a year or more on the tree. They tolerate partial shade and have a pleasing, rounded shape, attractive foliage and edible fruits, which means that they make good garden subjects, particularly in frost-free areas.

Although they are similar to the Criss-cross turkey-berry, **Rock-alder turkey-berries** (*C. mundianum*) have sparsely hairy leaves and their branches and leaves tend to be held horizontally. They occur from Cape Town, below the escarpment to Limpopo and westwards to Mahikeng. Outliers are found in Zimbabwe. These trees grow mostly in open, rocky areas, on termitaria, and in riparian scrub.

Rock-alder turkey-berry leaf upper-surface (***above***). Note the rounded shape and tapering base and apex. The petioles may be slightly twisted. On the leaf under-surface there are minute hairy pockets (***below***).

CG

Velvety turkey-berries have hairy leaves. The branches are not held as horizontally as in the Rock-alder turkey-berry.

Young stems of a **Criss-cross turkey-berry** showing the nearly opposite branches (which can become pointed and spine-like). Note the sheathing petiole. ***Inset top:*** Green and ripe fruits. The shape is typical for this genus. ***Inset bottom:*** Ripe fruits are very sweet and make good eating.

JB

Sand quar fruits. The leaves are very shiny and have undulating margins.

AS

Pioneer quar leaves are highly glossy. The tiny bumps are caused by the hairy pockets below.

JB

The trunk of a **Pioneer quar** is a useful identifying characteristic, as it is often fluted and twisted.

There are ~9 species of quar in the region. The two species that follow are typical of the genus:

Sand quars (*Psydrax locuples*) occur in coastal bushveld and thicket, often on sandy soils, from southern KwaZulu-Natal, along the Lebombo Mountains of Swaziland and Mozambique, and as far north as Maputo. The neat dark green leaves (20–45mm) have conspicuous pockets – they appear as tiny bumps from above.

Pioneer quars (*P. obovata*) are medium-sized trees found in forest and scrub from Swellendam as far north as Beira, as well as on the Lebombo Mountains and in eastern Zimbabwe. The trunks tend to be gnarled and slightly fluted, with rough blackish bark. The twigs are four-angled and the glossy leathery leaves (20–70 mm) have a round apex.

Crowned-medlars range in size from shrubs to small trees and are found in dry forest or bushveld habitats. The leaves lack pockets.

One example of the three crowned-medlars in the region is the **Forest crowned-medlar** (*Pachystigma bowkeri*), which has fissured grey bark and twigs, usually with conspicuous lenticels. The leaves are drooping, thinly textured, hairless, and can be bluish-green (30–150 mm).

Pioneer quars produce flowers in profusion. Note the exerted anthers.

RB

Forest crowned-medlars have drooping, thinly textured, hairless leaves.

Regionally there are ~25 species of bride's-bush. The genus and some species within it are not always easily distinguished. Most species range in size from shrubs to small trees and many grow in partly shaded situations. Blackish leaf nodules are generally common and conspicuous, but may sometimes be absent or widely scattered. All bride's-bushes have showy white flowers.

The **Dune bride's-bush** (*Pavetta revoluta*) occurs along the coast as a bush and occasionally a small tree, from Port Elizabeth to north of Maputo. The leaves tend to be thickish and leathery, with conspicuous pockets and slightly rolled margins. The leaf nodules are not always conspicuous.

Weeping bride's-bushes (*Pavetta lanceolata*) occur in forest, on forest edges and in wetter bushveld. They range in size from shrubs to small trees, and grow on sandy sites from Knysna to the Lebombo Mountains. The leaves are narrowly elliptic (35–100 mm), pliable, dark green above and dull below, with pockets and nodules.

Five bird-berries occur regionally. Some are large trees found in the forest understorey or at forest edges. Others are small shrubby trees with fairly large glossy leaves.

Forest bird-berries (*Psychotria capensis*) occur from Knysna to the Lebombo Mountains, and into eastern Zimbabwe. They grow in many forested habitats and even on rocky outcrops in grassland. The leaves (30–150 mm) are dark green, glossy, stiffly pliable, with conspicuous pockets and a rounded or bluntly tapering apex. There are 4–6 pairs of lateral veins.

Red bird-berries (*Psychotria zombamontana*) occur on the Lebombo Mountains and northern Drakensberg, in eastern Zimbabwe and into Mozambique. They are similar to Forest bird-berries, except that they have 10–16 pairs of lateral veins and the leaf upper-surfaces are distinctly quilted.

EvJ

Dune bride's-bush flowers have exaggerated extended pistils.

The leaf upper-surface of a **Dune bride's-bush** shows how the pockets below create bumps above. Note that the veins are unclear and the leaf apex is blunt.

Weeping bride's-bush leaf under-surface showing the rolled margins. ***Inset:*** Leaf under-surface showing the pockets in the axils. The larger lumps in the middle of the blade are nitrogen-fixing bacterial nodules (see arrow).

Forest bird-berry with fruits. Note the broad, smooth, glossy leaves with partly obscured lateral veins.

Twig of a **Red bird-berry** showing the diagnostic, slightly looping lateral veins.

Notes

- Bride's-bushes and bird-berries are great garden shrubs, preferring partial shade but able to grow in full sun if kept moist. They are tough and can thrive in many climatic zones. With their glossy or highly glossy leaves and showy flowers they make attractive garden subjects.

Monkey-orange Family

Loganiaceae

~400 spp. globally; ~30 spp. regionally, all trees

BW

The **Corky-bark monkey-orange** is named for its thick corky bark, which protects the tree from bush fires.

HFG

Corky-bark monkey-orange leaves are typical for the genus: they are simple, opposite, entire and shiny, with 3–7 veins running from the base of the leaf.

HFG

The large, finely textured, wooden fruit of a **Corky-bark monkey-orange** is typical of many bushveld species in this genus.

The following family characteristics are used for identification purposes:

- ✓ leaves simple, opposite or whorled
- ✓ stipules can be reduced and sometimes there is an interpetiolar stipular line
- ✓ at least three-veined from the base, with entire leaf margins

Strychnos is an important genus in this family and includes the monkey-oranges, which have large (60–120 mm), very woody fruits, and the bitterberries, which have small, soft and fleshy fruits. There are ~17 *Strychnos* spp. in the region, most of which are small to medium-sized trees:

Corky-bark monkey-oranges (*S. cocculoides*) are a widespread monkey-orange species and occur in bushveld, usually on sandy soils or rocky hills from northcentral South Africa into Zimbabwe and westwards to Owambo in Namibia. They are small compact trees with a rounded canopy and corky bark. The leaves are almost round, with a sharp leaf tip, and 3–7 veins running from the base. Scattered, strong, paired, curved spines are also a distinguishing feature. The fruits are hard with a woody shell, about 70 mm in diameter, dark green, and speckled with white.

Spiny monkey-oranges (*S. spinosa*) are similar, but the leaves are five-veined from the base, the stems bear spines that are mostly straight, and the fruits are ~100 mm in diameter and slightly warty, with very faint speckles. The bark is smoothish. They occur in bushveld along the east coast from East London to the Zambezi, westwards to Mahikeng and through Zimbabwe to Owambo in Namibia.

AS (main pic)

The **Spiny monkey-orange** fruit is a conspicuous woody ball that is light green and turns yellow when ripe. ***Inset:*** As the name implies, small to quite stout spines can occur on the twigs. The leaves may have more than three basal veins.

The **Spiny-leaved monkey-orange** (*S. pungens*) has much more rigid leaves that are spine-tipped; otherwise these small bushveld trees are spineless. The fruits measure <122 mm and are bluish-green to yellow when ripe. They occur in Limpopo and the North West province in South Africa, in the central parts of southern Zimbabwe and from Caprivi to Owambo in Namibia.

Depending on habitat, **Black monkey-oranges** (*S. madagascariensis*) vary in size: the forest form grows into a large tree, while specimens that grow in bushveld, in sandy areas and on rocky sites are smaller. Both forms have smooth bluish fruits of ~70 mm in diameter. Bushveld trees have leaves with rounded apices borne on stubby dwarf twigs. In the forest form, the leaves are more elliptic, with tapering apices.

The following two bitterberries are fairly common in the region:

The **Cape-teak bitterberry** (*S. decussata*) grows in coastal and low-altitude afromontane forest and in bushveld, from Knysna to the Lebombo Mountains and in northern Zimbabwe. The leaves overlap along the midrib, but it is the dark, almost bluish-brown bark, which is minutely cracked and fissured, that is most distinctive.

Blue bitterberries (*S. usambarensis*) have leaf apices that taper almost to a drip-tip. These trees occur from north of East London to northern KwaZulu-Natal and inland to Mahikeng, as well as in eastern Zimbabwe. They are found in forest and mixed bushveld in rocky areas.

HFG

The leaves of the **Spiny-leaved monkey-orange** are very hard and have tough spiny tips – hence this tree's common name.

The leaves of **Black monkey-oranges** occur on stiff stubby shoots. In bushveld specimens the leaves have rounded apices.

Black monkey-orange fruits and leaves have a bluish tinge.

Cape-teak bitterberry leaves can have tiny mucros. The basal lateral veins tend to loop along the leaf margins.

TA

Blue bitterberry leaves tend to have a much longer, more tapering tip than is usual for the bitterberries.

Notes

- The fleshy covering of the seeds of the woody-fruited monkey-orange species can be delicious. Some rural people peel this off, dry the flesh and then use it to make flour.
- It's important to note that the kernel of the seed can be very poisonous as it contains varying quantities of strychnine, hence the generic name *Strychnos*.

Oleander Family

Apocynaceae

~1 500 spp. globally; ~40 spp. regionally, ~25 spp. of tree

Ripe black fruits of the **Bushman's poison-bush**. The leaves are stiff, leathery and opaque, with slightly raised lateral veins, and have a sharply pointed spout-like tip. Note the yellowish margins. ***Inset:*** The flowers are sweet-smelling, star-shaped and can occur in profusion.

Amatungulu num-num leaves are tough and glossy with a mucro. The spines can be twice divided, but are usually forked.

TA

Amatungulu num-num fruits turn from green to dark red when ripe. The ripe fruits are edible. ***Inset:*** The flowers are larger than those of other num-nums.

This is an easily recognised family of mostly woody species that have the following characteristics:

- ✓ leaves simple, glossy, opposite or whorled, margins entire (rarely alternate)
- ✓ milky latex – usually copious, but sometimes more watery than milky
- ✓ fruits often in pairs (with a few notable exceptions)

Bushman's poison-bush (*Acokanthera oppositifolia*) is a shrub or small tree found in many habitats, including riparian bush, on termitaria in bushveld and on forest edges. It is found from Cape Agulhas to Limpopo at lower altitudes, and westwards to Mahikeng, as well as in central and eastern Zimbabwe. The leaves are thick and very leathery, elliptic, broadly tapering with a spiny tip. The petioles can be purplish and the flowers are in tight bunches, white and sweetly scented. The fruit is ovoid, fleshy, turning red to purplish-black when ripe.

The 6 num-num species are mostly shrubs, all strongly spinescent and similar-looking. The only tree-like species among them is the **Amatungulu num-num** (*Carissa macrocarpa*), which has Y-shaped spines up to 45 mm long. This species has larger flowers (25–50 mm) and fruits than other num-nums (ovoid, up to 40 mm). The fruits turn red to purple as they ripen. This species occurs from Mossel Bay northwards into southern Mozambique and westwards to Mahikeng, with some scattered populations in Zimbabwe.

Gonioma is a monotypic genus: it includes just one species, the **Forest kamassi** (*G. kamassi*), which is a small subcanopy tree found in afromontane forest from Knysna (where it can be common) to Durban and occasionally on the Lebombo Mountains. The leaves are mostly four-whorled, narrowly elliptic and glossy.

A **Forest kamassi** twig showing the whorled leaf arrangement. The leaves are light green with inconspicuous lateral veins. ***Inset:*** Young green fruits together with the hard capsules of some old fruits that have opened to release the winged seeds. The light ribbing on the surface of the capsules becomes more prominent as they dry.

The **Bushveld horn-pod tree** (*Diplorhynchus condylocarpon*) occurs on stony hillsides in bushveld. These small trees have slender hanging branches. The leaves are opposite, elliptic and drooping, with margins that may be wavy, and with yellowish lateral veins. The combination of warty fruits, habitat and distribution confirms this tree's identity. In South Africa it occurs in northern bushveld areas often on sandy soils. It also occurs throughout most of Zimbabwe, westwards through northern Botswana and Caprivi, and into northern Namibia.

The small neat **Warty-fruited toad-tree** (*Tabernaemontana elegans*) grows in riparian bush and on the edges of coastal forest. These trees are found along the KwaZulu-Natal coastal fringe to Swaziland, in the northern Kruger National Park and in Zimbabwe's eastern highlands. They are easily recognised by the paired warty fruits, which hang from the twigs. The leaves tend to be crowded towards the twig ends and are thinly leathery and glossy, with conspicuous lateral veins. The corky, deeply fissured, creamy brown bark is also characteristic.

The **Smooth-fruited toad-tree** (*T. ventricosa*) occurs on forest edges and in the forest subcanopy from north of Durban to the eastern highlands of Zimbabwe. This medium-sized tree has smooth paired fruits.

GN (both)

Smooth-fruited toad-tree fruits split open revealing the seeds and bright yellow pulp. ***Inset:*** Flowers are produced at the edge of the canopy.

BW

Bushveld horn-pods have thick corky bark that has a blocky appearance.

TC

Bushveld horn-pods have diagnostic paired pendulous fruits with lightly warty skin. The leaves turn yellow before falling.

NC

The most diagnostic feature of the **Warty-fruited toad-tree** is its bumpy fruits, which hang in fixed pairs. ***Inset above:*** The veins are far more prominent below the leaf than above. ***Inset left:*** The trunk has thick corky bark, unlike that of the Smooth-fruited toad-tree, which has smooth bark.

Notes

- The unripe fruits of Bushman's poison-bush and its close relative the Dune poison-bush (which has spirally alternate leaves, sometimes subopposite) are deadly poisonous. Even ripe fruits should be avoided.
- Bushmen used the latex of Bushman's poison-bush as one of the ingredients for their deadly poison-tipped arrows.

The **African wild-frangipane** (*Voacanga thouarsii*) is a medium-sized to large tree that occurs in moist areas such as swamp forest, along river banks, and on forest margins. It is found from southern KwaZulu-Natal to Maputo and in the Zambezi delta. The leaves are opposite, dark green, glossy, clustered apically, and have rounded apices. The petioles join to form a cup-like structure or sheath. The flowers are white to yellow and up to 45 mm in diameter.

African quinine-trees (*Rauvolfia caffra*) can be quite large. They occur in frost-free areas from Port St Johns to Swaziland, west almost to Mahikeng and north to the Limpopo. They are also found in central and eastern Zimbabwe. They always grow close to water, in swamp forest and in riparian communities. The bark is yellowish to brown, corky and longitudinally fissured, cracking into small rectangles. The leaves are in whorls of 3–6. They are bright green, pliable, glossy, elliptic with a tapering base and tip (100–200 mm), and have conspicuous lateral veins. The flowers are tiny and borne in dense sprays, while the fruits are mostly single, round (5–20 mm), and green with white spots.

African saddle-pods (*Wrightia natalensis*) are medium-sized trees found in dry forest and on hillsides. They are uncommon and occur from Port St Johns northwards along the Lebombo Mountains into southern Zimbabwe. The leaves are drooping, narrowly elliptic (35–95 mm) and light green. The slender, twinned pods may be as long as 300 mm.

BP

Mature fruits of the **African wild-frangipane** have a blotchy appearance. Note the rounded tips to the leaves and the large leaf scars on the twig.

BP

The petioles of **African wild-frangipane** join up, forming a sheath on the stem (see arrow).

The apical tip of an **African quinine-tree** showing the glossy narrowly elliptic leaves ***(above)***. Note that the plant is exuding milky latex where a leaf has been removed ***(below)***.

GN

HFG

The **African saddle-pod** gets its name from its fruits, which are two long capsules joined together ***(left)***. The seeds inside the open fruit have silky plumes to assist with wind dispersion ***(right)***.

The **Richtersveld halfmens** (*Pachypodium namaquanum*) has a single succulent stem that is covered with spines. The leaves occur in an apical rosette, which makes these trees conspicuous and easy to identify. They occur in the Richtersveld and just north of the Orange River into southern Namibia.

Namibian bottle-trees (*P. lealii*) occur in northern Kaokoland as thick succulent trees up to 6 m tall. They are bottle shaped, with scattered spines and an apical rosettes of leaves.

The **Namibian bottle-tree** has far fewer spines on its trunk than the Richtersveld halfmens and is sparsely branched.

JB

The **Richtersveld halfmens** grows in hostile terrain and is easy to identify by its spine-covered trunk and apical rosette of leaves. ***Inset:*** A close-up of the stem apex showing the flowers, undulating leaf margins and spines.

INTRODUCED SPECIES: Oleanders (*Nerium oleander*) originated in the Atlas Mountains.They can withstand harsh and dry environments, so have been widely cultivated and are often planted as barrier plants along roads This toxic species has escaped and now occurs along some Western Cape rivers.

Left: Stem detail of an **Oleander** showing the leaf bases. ***Right:*** A pink-flowered form. Note the whorled leaves.

Forget-me-not Family

Boraginaceae ~2 000 spp. globally; ~80 spp. regionally, ~10 spp. of tree

This is a family of mainly herbaceous plants. The tree species can be recognised by the following characteristics:

- ✓ simple alternate leaves that are often sandpapery
- ✓ no stipules
- ✓ twig ends tend to be rounded

The leaves of the 8 species of saucer-bush (*Cordia* spp.) give off an aromatic 'green-leaf' smell when crushed. The fruits are characteristically fleshy, one-seeded and partially or completely surrounded by a persistent enlarged calyx cup. The young twigs and leaves are often hairy.

A medium-sized, well-branched tree, the **Large-leaved saucer-bush** (*C. africana*) is found in bushveld in northern Kaokoland, around Musina in Limpopo, and in Zimbabwe along the Great Dyke and in the eastern highlands. The leaves are wide at the base, three-veined, pliable and, particularly when young, roughly textured. These trees are conspicuous when in flower and fruit.

The **Septee saucer-bush** (*C. caffra*) is medium-sized with mottled light brown bark that flakes off in large pieces. The tree is often a little crooked. Its drooping leaves (50–100 mm) are thinly textured and tend to rotate in the wind. It occurs in dry coastal forest, on forest edges and in riparian bush from East London to northern KwaZulu-Natal and along the Lebombo Mountains.

HFG (inset: BW)

A **Large-leaved saucer-bush** is conspicuous when in flower. ***Inset:*** The fruits become yellow as they ripen.

HFG

Left: **Septee saucer-bush trees** have smooth light brown bark that peels off in sizeable pieces. ***Centre:*** A fruiting twig showing the characteristic long pendent petioles and typical leaf shape. Note the unequal leaf bases and the attenuated apex. ***Right:*** The fruits have a persistent cup-shaped calyx.

Satin-bark saucer-bushes (*C. ovalis*) range from multi-branched shrubs to small trees. They grow at low altitudes in sandy or alluvial areas in the bushveld. Their range extends from KwaZulu-Natal to Limpopo, and they also occur in northeastern Zimbabwe and northern Namibia. The leaves are almost round (30–90 mm). The upper-surface is leathery, harsh and bristly, but the yellowish under-surface is smoother.

The 7 species of puzzle-bush (*Ehretia* spp.) have leaves that are usually hairless and a little sandpapery and that give off a pungent odour when crushed. Their fruits are small and fleshy. Generally they are shrubs, but the following may grow into small trees:

The **Deurmekaar puzzle-bush** (*E. rigida*) ranges in size from a rigid woody shrub to a small tree. It is widespread in bushveld and karoo west and north of Port Elizabeth, and extends to southeastern Zimbabwe and eastwards to Kosi Bay. The leaves (20–60 mm) are crowded on short rigid branches, and are characterised by sandpapery margins – gently feel for this with your tongue.

Sandpaper puzzle-bushes (*E. amoena*) occur in bushveld, mopane vegetation and along drainage lines from northern KwaZulu-Natal to northcentral Zimbabwe and east to the coast of Mozambique. They are twiggy shrubs or small trees with arching branches. Both leaf surfaces are a little sandpapery.

TW

Sandpaper puzzle-bushes have sandpapery leaves and bear many fleshy red fruits **(*above*)**. They produce masses of tiny, sweet-smelling white flowers **(*below*)**.

BW

TW (inset: LL)

Satin-bark saucer-bushes have rounded leathery leaves. The fruits are typical for the genus. ***Inset:*** The bark flakes to reveal diagnostic smooth bluish-green bark resembling that of a gum tree.

JB

The **Deurmekaar puzzle-bush** has small flowers. The leaves, which have sandpapery margins, are often bunched at the ends of the short twigs.

JB

Deurmekaar puzzle-bush fruits have the persistent calyx that is typical of the family, but differ in being lobed, not saucer-shaped.

Nightshade Family

Solanaceae

~2 000 spp. globally; ~50 spp. regionally, ~10 spp. of tree

Like many members of this family, the **Kraal honey-thorn** often bears its flowers and fruits at the same time. Note that the leaves of this tree are rounder and more succulent than those of most other *Lycium* spp.

River honey-thorn leaves are tiny and occur mostly on dwarf shoots.

A vegetatively diverse family. Its members may tend to become weeds. Some distinctive family features are:

- ✓ leaves simple, alternate (or spirally arranged), without stipules
- ✓ when crushed, leaves often give off an unpleasant smell
- ✓ a number of species are spiny
- ✓ fruit is a many-seeded berry (or capsule)

There are ~9 species of honey-thorn regionally – all difficult to distinguish. They tend to have small soft or slightly fleshy leaves (<50 mm), usually carried in apical bunches, short spine-tipped branches, bell-shaped greenish flowers, and small (~10 mm), soft, yellow to red fruits.

The **Kraal honey-thorn** (*Lycium afrum*) is largely restricted to coastal scrub in the Western Cape where it can grow into a small tree (4–5 m).

The **River honey-thorn** (*L. hirsutum*) has drooping branches and hairy leaves and occurs in the Karoo, often on calcareous soils and along stream banks.

There are two species of bitter-apples regionally, both with large softish leaves that are whitish and woolly below.

Goat bitter-apples (*Solanum aculeastrum*) range in size from shrubs to small trees and are very spiny – even the leaf under-surfaces carry spines. The leaves are large (45–140 mm) and lobed. They occur on slopes and forest edges from Mossel Bay to the Lebombos and in eastern Zimbabwe. The species is a weed in disturbed areas, where it can occur in dense colonies.

Healing-leaf bitter-apples (*S. giganteum*) have stout spines (<10 mm). The leaves are dark green, well lobed and entire (70–300 mm). The twigs and leaf under-surfaces carry dense white hairs. The fruits are bright red (~10 mm). These trees occur on mountain slopes or in forest clearings from Knysna northwards, skirt the central grasslands, and extend west to Mahikeng. Also found in eastern Zimbabwe.

EvJ

CV

Pale flowers ***(left)*** and fruit ***(top)*** of a young **Goat bitter-apple**.

Healing-leaf bitter-apples produce fruits that are sought-after by birds.

GG

INTRODUCED SPECIES: A number of introduced species have become naturalised. **Bugweed** (*Solanum mauritianum*), originally introduced from Asia, is now widespread in disturbed forest, on hillsides in higher rainfall areas, and along drainage lines and roadsides. The hairy grey-green leaves (100–250 mm) are woolly below, as are the twigs. The fruits are ~10 mm long and turn yellow when ripe.

Inkberry (*Cestrum laevigatum*) originated in South America and has become a widespread weed of the tropics and subtropics. It has light green foliage and tubular creamy yellow flowers. The leaves emit a strong unpleasant aroma when crushed. Inkberry is becoming troublesome in disturbed areas along the east coast of southern Africa from East London northwards.

Wild tobacco (*Nicotiana glauca*) is another South American plant that has become a weed in many parts of the region (except for the Kalahari). It is a slender tree, often most visible in arid areas along drainage lines, on roadsides and in other disturbed areas. The distinctive shape of this small tree, the blue-green leaves, and masses of small, tubular yellowish flowers make it easily identifiable.

Ripe **Bugweed** fruits resemble yellow cocktail tomatoes and are highly sought-after by frugivorous birds.

Bugweed trees bear flowers and, later, fruits on flattened inflorescences held slightly above the canopy (***above***). **Wild tobacco** flowers and fruits (***below***).

Inkberry flowers smell sweet and are an inconspicuous pale greenish-yellow. The crushed leaves emit a pungent odour.

Wild tobacco typically grows on steep slopes, in disturbed areas and along seasonal watercourses.

Notes

- Many species in the nightshade family are able to spread into a wide range of habitats and have a tendency to become weeds. They have become far more widespread in recent times.
- A number of species in the family are important food plants, including potatoes, tomatoes, chillies and peppers.

Olive Family

Oleaceae

~600 spp. globally; ~15 spp. regionally, ~10 spp. of tree

Wing-leaved wooden-pears are most conspicuous in full fruit. Here the winged seeds have been released, leaving the wooden capsules empty. ***Inset:*** Flowers and pinnately compound leaves. The rachis is slightly winged.

In some years **Forest pock-ironwoods** fruit heavily. This individual has fairly inconspicuous leaf bumps.

The **Forest pock-ironwood** can have very conspicuous bumps on the leaf upper-surface, created by pockets in the axils of the veins below. The leaves are stiff with rolled margins.

This mainly woody family is not easy to characterise vegetatively. Look for a combination of the following features:

- ✓ leaves, simple or pinnately compound, opposite or subopposite
- ✓ margins entire
- ✓ no stipules
- ✓ twigs always with a few whitish lenticels

The genera and species, however, are more easily identified.

The **Wing-leaved wooden-pear** (*Schrebera alata*) is a small to medium-sized tree with imparipinnate leaves that have a diagnostic winged rachis. When in fruit, the pear-shaped, upright, light brown woody capsules (25–35 mm long) are also diagnostic. These trees occur in bushveld on rocky outcrops, forest edges and even in dry forest from the Pondoland coast to the Limpopo River and westwards to Mahikeng. They also occur in central and eastern Zimbabwe to Beira.

Named for the usually conspicuous pockets that are found in the axils of the veins below the leaves, **Forest pock-ironwoods** (*Chionanthus foveolatus*) also have obvious raised bumps on the leaf upper-surfaces. These trees have pale bark and can grow quite large, although they are most often seen as slender subcanopy saplings in forests, where they have a few stiff leaves, many held horizontally. They also occur as leafy shrubs in rocky outcrops or on forest edges, where their leaves tend to be more upright. The species occurs in afromontane forest from Cape Town to northern KwaZulu-Natal, and into Mpumalanga, Gauteng, Limpopo and as far north as the Chimanimani Mountains.

The **African olive** (*Olea europaea*) is another easily recognised member of this family. The leaves are narrowly elliptic and bicoloured: olive-green and slightly glossy above, dull to whitish-buff, even yellowish, below. On old trees the leaves tend to droop. The lateral veins that join to form a squiggly vein just inside the rolled-over margin are indistinct. The African olive is one of the most widely occurring trees in South Africa, Zimbabwe and the central highlands of Namibia. It grows in many habitats: in bushveld, on termitaria, in forest and on forest edges, on rocky sites and even inland on sandy sites, but is absent from desert areas.

Dune olives (*O. exasperata*) are similar, but the leaves are paler green, not as distinctly bicoloured, and the leaf tips arch backwards. They are restricted to sandy soils along the west coast from Saldanha to Port Elizabeth.

There are two subspecies of **Forest ironwood** (*O. capensis*) that are fairly easy to identify. One is a giant with leathery elliptic leaves (40–100 mm), which is found in afromontane forests in South Africa. The other subspecies occurs in rocky mountainous sites from the Western Cape to north of East London, often on forest edges, and is a small tree with much stiffer, rounder leaves that have a hard, almost pointed, spout-like tip.

A very old and gnarled **African olive** in dry forest. Note the many tiny coppice shoots. Tree trunks like this are often home to a variety of animals. ***Inset:*** Young fruiting twigs are whitish. The leaves are olive green.

The non-forest form of **Forest ironwood** in full flower. ***Inset:*** The leaves of the non-forest form are much rounder and stiffer than those of the forest form, and have a spout-like leaf tip.

A **Dune olive** twig showing the opposite to sub-opposite leaf arrangement, the reflexed tips, strongly rolled margins and inconspicuous lateral veins.

Dune olive in full fruit.

The bark of this **Forest ironwood,** which has been growing in wet forest, is covered in epiphytic mosses and lichens.

Notes

- Evidence from the Mediterranean suggests that African olives were among the earliest plants domesticated. Until fairly recently, Mediterranean and southern African olives were recognised as separate species. However, research has shown that they are one species.
- The timber of the Forest ironwood is valued for making furniture.

Nuxia family

Stilbaceae

~20 spp. globally; ~14 spp. regionally, ~7 spp. of tree

BW

The many tiny four-petalled flowers in the inflorescence of a **Brittlewood nuxia** are typical of the genus.

BW

Three-whorled coppice leaves of a **Brittlewood nuxia**. Note the reddish stems of the soft young twigs.

In full flower **Forest nuxias** are conspicuous and attractive.

The characteristics of this essentially southern African endemic family of woody plants include:

- ✓ leaves opposite or whorled
- ✓ petioles forming an urn-shaped junction with the twig

There are some five nuxia species and, as a rule, they have three-whorled leaves.

Brittlewood nuxias (*Nuxia congesta*) range in size from shrubs to large trees. They occupy dry positions within coastal and afromontane forests, and rocky positions in bushveld and grassland. They occur in a band from East London to the border of Mozambique and eastwards through northern South Africa as far as Mahikeng. They also occur in northeastern Zimbabwe. The plant and leaves are variable, although the leaves tend to be crowded at the twig ends and the twigs themselves typically have 6–8 ridges. The leaf margins are usually entire, except on coppice shoots.

Forest nuxias (*N. floribunda*) are medium-sized forest or forest-edge trees. The leaves are opposite or three-whorled, elliptic (50–120 mm), with long slender petioles (15–40 mm). The margins are entire, except for those on coppice shoots. The petioles and young twigs may be purplish.

Coppice shoots of the **Forest nuxia**: the internodes and leaves are well spread out. In older trees the internodes are closer and the leaves bunch terminally.

Left: **Forest nuxias** have long petioles that occur in whorls of three. ***Right:*** **Water nuxias** have opposite leaves and the young stems may be quite reddish and angular.

Left: **Rock tree-fuchsia** showing that the petioles form an urn-shaped juncture. ***Right:*** **African pambatis** have woolly twigs and petioles.

Water nuxias (*N. oppositifolia*) are multi-stemmed shrubs or small willow-like trees found along drainage lines, in riparian situations and even among boulders. They occur from KwaZulu-Natal northwards, in a broad arc into Zimbabwe and eastwards to Beira, with outliers in northern Kaokoland. The leaves are mainly opposite, occasionally three-whorled, narrowly oblong, with a shallowly toothed margin.

Rock tree-fuchsias (*Halleria lucida*) are among the most easily identifiable trees in the region, being small to medium-sized with long, tubular, showy orange to red flowers produced on old wood. The leaves are characteristically opposite, minutely toothed, and drooping. They occur from Cape Town eastwards, below the escarpment and west to Mahikeng, and in the northern parts of Zimbabwe's eastern highlands. They grow in forest, on forest edges, in riparian situations and in rocky outcrops at altitude, but not in bushveld.

African pambatis (*Anastrabe integerrima*) are small trees and shrubs found in riparian areas and on forest edges below the escarpment from Port Elizabeth to northern KwaZulu-Natal. They can be identified by their stiff dark green leaves, which are yellowish and woolly below, and by their cup-shaped yellow flowers.

The **African pambati** has characteristic small yellow flowers and serrate leaves, although in some specimens the leaves are entire.

Water nuxias typically have ribbon-like leaves and tiny white flowers.

Rock tree-fuchsias are easy to identify precisely, as they bear their flowers and fruit on old wood. ***Inset:*** The leaves are finely serrate, with a lightly quilted upper-surface, attenuated apex and broad base.

Notes

- Until recently this family was considered a fynbos endemic, its only members being a few small woody shrubs. However, recent DNA studies have placed the nuxias, tree-fuchsias and African pambati in this family, thus more than doubling the number of genera.
- Many of the tree-sized species in this family are good garden subjects because they do not grow too large.
- Tree-fuchsias attract sunbirds when in flower and frugivorous birds when in fruit.

Jacaranda Family

Bignoniaceae

~700 spp. globally; ~11 spp. regionally, ~8 spp. of tree

A huge **African sausage-tree** in the Kruger National Park.

The fruits of the **African sausage-tree** can weigh more than 10 kg. Elephants disperse the seeds.

African sausage-tree flowers, which are large and fairly well hidden within the foliage, are bat pollinated.

A distinctive family of both woody and herbaceous species. The following are some distinguishing features:

- ✓ pinnately compound, opposite or whorled leaves without stipules
- ✓ flowers are large, bell- or funnel-shaped and showy
- ✓ fruits in many species can resemble a pod and split open when ripe
- ✓ many species have seeds with membranous wings

This family includes the iconic **African sausage-tree** (*Kigelia africana*), which occurs from KwaZulu-Natal eastwards and northwards to Caprivi and beyond. It is a medium to large tree found in riparian areas and tall bushveld. The heavy, sausage-like fruits are diagnostic (200–350 mm), as are the imparipinnate leaves and large deep maroon flowers (60–80 mm in diameter), which hang on a loose spike, usually hidden inside the tree.

The **Cape honeysuckle** (*Tecomaria capensis*) is common, widespread and often cultivated. It ranges in size from a scrambling shrub to a small tree and grows in the bushveld and at forest edges from around Cape Agulhas to the Lebombo Mountains and the southern coast of Mozambique. The flowers, usually present throughout the year, are distinctive. In the wild most are bright orange, but they can range from almost white to red.

Cape honeysuckles have hairy pockets in the axils of the veins on the leaf under-surfaces (***above***). This is a scrambling tree that is a common and widespread horticultural subject and readily forms a hedge (***left***).

The genus *Rhigozum* mainly comprises species that are spiny shrubs and small trees. The most robust is the **Mopane rhigozum** (*Rhigozum zambesiacum*), which occurs from northern KwaZulu-Natal, along the Lebombo Mountains and into the Limpopo River valley, as well as in the Zambezi valley in northern Zimbabwe. It occurs in low-altitude bushveld and in rocky situations. The branches tend to be sub-opposite and the leaves are imparipinnate (7–11 leaflets, 10–30 mm long) and clustered on spur-like twiglets. The flowers are golden yellow and showy (~35 mm in diameter) and the fruit is a flat, smooth, slender, lightly woody capsule that splits into two, releasing winged seeds.

Zambezi pink-jacarandas (*Stereospermum kunthianum*) are generally medium sized and grow mainly on termitaria in riparian bush, or on rocky sites and hills in bushveld in the greater Zambezi valley. The flowers, which are borne in large sprays, are a showy pink with red streaks. The fruit is a slender, flat, woody capsule. They have been named 'jacaranda' as they superficially resemble the cultivated jacaranda.

JB

Mopane rhigozum capsules split into two to release their winged seeds.

DP

TW

JB

The **Mopane rhigozum** is a hard prickly shrub with fairly dense foliage and opposite twigs. ***Inset:*** The butter yellow flowers make an attractive show in spring.

Zambezi pink-jacarandas bear large sprays of pink flowers during spring.

INTRODUCED SPECIES: The widely cultivated **Jacaranda** (*Jacaranda mimosifolia*), introduced from the high Andes, has been extensively planted for shade and for the mass of purple flowers it produces in spring, when the tree is leafless. Jacarandas have become naturalised in subtropical areas, in forest, on hill slopes and in riparian bush. They are deemed a pest.

Jacarandas have feathery, bipinnately compound leaves, but it is the flowers that make this species easy to identify.

Mint Family

Lamiaceae

~6 900 spp. globally; ~75 spp. regionally, ~15 spp. of tree

BW

Smelly-berry fingerleaves have long thin petioles and a rounded leaf tip.

JEB

Kei fingerleaf twig showing the backs of the leaves, which have conspicuous looping veins.

BW

Chocolate-berry fingerleaves have prominent veins on both leaf surfaces. They are densely hairy below.

Trees in the (mainly herbaceous) mint family are not easy to distinguish vegetatively, but the following are helpful characteristics:

- ✓ leaves are opposite or whorled
- ✓ leaves can be simple or palmately compound (rarely trifoliolate)
- ✓ crushed leaves are often strongly aromatic (sometimes unpleasantly so)

There are ~14 species of fingerleaf, generally with palmately compound leaves, mostly deciduous shrubs or small trees in bushveld.

Smelly-berry fingerleaves (*Vitex mombassae*) occur mainly on Kalahari sands in northern Botswana and central Zimbabwe. Leaves can be 3–5-foliolate with slender petioles and the lower leaflets may be small or absent. They tend to be yellowish-green, have prominent veins and are covered in short hairs that are densest below.

Kei fingerleaves (*V. obovata*) occur from Grahamstown to northeastern KwaZulu-Natal and on the northern Lebombo Mountains, often in dry, stony bushveld sites. The leaflets have 4–7 mm-long petioles and are yellow-green or khaki with velvety under-surfaces.

Chocolate-berry fingerleaves (*V. payos*) are restricted largely to bushveld vegetation in Zimbabwe. They are medium-sized trees with a rounded crown. The leaflets are almost sessile, bright green and finely hairy with a quilted look, and the under-surfaces are reddish and woolly.

African timberwoods (*Clerodendrum glabrum*) can be recognised by the pungent odour of their crushed leaves. The leaves are three-whorled, broadly elliptic and drooping, with entire margins and longish petioles (10–25 mm). They are widespread in many habitats from rocky areas in bushveld, to forest edges and rocky outcrops in eastern grassland habitat. They occur from East London along the coast and below the escarpment into eastern Botswana and Zimbabwe, with outliers in northern Namibia along the Cunene River.

African timberwood with green fruits. The leaves are paler below with slightly wavy margins and have a tapering apex.

AS

Rough-leaved cats-whiskers (*Rotheca myricoides*) are shrubs to small trees. They grow in rocky areas and thickets in bushveld vegetation, from southern KwaZulu-Natal through Swaziland and westwards to Mahikeng, as well as in central and northern Zimbabwe. The leaves are clustered on the twig ends and are usually twice as long as they are broad (25–70 mm), velvety above, woolly below, with a tapering base that runs down the petiole.

Chinese-hats are separated geographically, with **Southern Chinese-hats** (*Karomia speciosa*) occurring in the Swaziland area and along the Lebombo Mountains, and **Northern Chinese-hats** (*K. tettensis*) in the Zambezi valley. They are identified by their flowers, which have a pink-to-mauve saucer-shaped calyx and a bright blue corolla.

GG

GG

Rough-leaved cats-whiskers may have three-whorled, opposite or sub-opposite leaves on the same plant **(*above*)**. This side view of the flower shows the recurved stamens and style **(*left*)**.

Southern Chinese-hats get their common name from their purple flowers, which have a large pink calyx.

RE

Northern Chinese-hat leaves have a dentate margin and end in a mucro.

INTRODUCED SPECIES: The highly invasive prickly shrub **Lantana** (*Lantana camara*), which occurs in subtropical and tropical bushveld and dry forest, belongs to a closely allied family Verbenaceae. This is an invasive species of global significance. It is a particular problem on many islands and in Australia. In Africa it can act as a pioneer in badly degraded areas, holding the soil and acting as a nurse plant by providing shade and protection to seedlings. However, its pest plant status is compounded by the fact that it is toxic to cattle.

Lantanas bear dense heads of showy, brightly coloured flowers.

Notes

- Many species in this family are used for flavouring food, e.g. mint, basil, sage, rosemary and thyme.
- Oils are extracted from other aromatic members of the family, such as lavender. Chia (tea) is another well-known member of the Lamiaceae.

Daisy Family

Asteraceae ~23 000 spp. globally; ~2 400 spp. regionally, ~22 spp. of tree

This huge family of mostly herbaceous plants is the ninth largest tree family in the region. Some of the woody species have separate male and female trees. The woody species in the region are most easily identified at the genus level:

- ✓ the diagnostic feature of this family is the typical daisy 'flower' (actually an inflorescence)

The silver-oaks, of which ~9 species occur in the region, are widespread through many habitats. This is the second largest tree genus in the family. Most species are small to medium-sized evergreen trees. They all have bicoloured, simple, spirally arranged leaves that are glossy and dark green above, whitish and woolly below, with edges that are generally not entire.

Coastal silver-oaks (*Brachylaena discolor*) are arguably the best known, occurring in dune forest as straggling trees. They have glossy, very dark green leaves, with white under-surfaces and spiky edges. The blackish branches (which have scattered white lenticels) make good spear shafts and fishing rods. These features are diagnostic.

Cape silver-oaks (*B. neriifolia*) are fynbos endemics and are usually riparian. The leaves are narrowly elliptic, generally with entire edges that roll under slightly, and the under-surface is off-white.

Coastal silver-oaks form very dense tangles and barriers where they occur *en masse*.

Coastal silver-oaks have uneven, glossy to highly glossy dark green leaf upper-surfaces. The margins may be spiky. The twigs are covered in matted white hairs.

The spiky female flowers of the **Coastal silver-oak** are visited by bees.

EvJ

Cape silver-oak twig and fruits. Note the paler and densely hairy leaf under-surface.

The leaves of the **Cape silver-oak** are clustered apically and are more serrate in the outer third.

Bitter-leaf silver-oaks (*B. elliptica*) range in size from shrubs to small trees and occur in coastal and riparian bush, as well as in bushveld at lower altitudes from Knysna to north of Maputo. The leaf apices are broadly tapering or rounded and may even have two lobes, while the leaf edges vary from spiky to entire.

Lowveld silver-oaks (*B. huillensis*) are small trees that occur in dry areas, on rocky sites and in sandy soils. The leaves tend to be crowded apically and can have a broadly tapering apex and sharp bristle tip. The edges are entire and roll under slightly. These trees occur in northern KwaZulu-Natal, on the Lebombo Mountains and as far west as Mahikeng, as well as along the border of and into southern and eastern Zimbabwe.

Small-leaved silver-oaks (*B. ilicifolia*) are shrubs to small trees that occur in rocky situations or on hills in bushveld. The leaves are small, crowded (10–40 mm) and are sometimes borne on little twigs.

JEB

Lowveld silver-oak female flowers. Note the white under-surfaces of the leaves.

HFG

Small-leaved silver-oak female flowers.

GG

Leaves of a **Bitter-leaf silver-oak**: note the leaf that has been turned over to show the whitish under-surface.

JB

A **Lowveld silver-oak** with old flowers.

Notes

- With the exception of the distinctive Cape silver-oak, silver-oaks can be difficult to distinguish from one another because their leaf morphology is so variable – as is often the case with members of the daisy family. For this reason, habitat and distribution are important for identification.
- Coastal silver-oaks are exceptionally wind resistant. They grow quickly in warm frost-free environments. They may coppice prolifically and are, therefore, useful barrier plants where large hedges are required.

The genus *Vernonia*, found in wetter habitats, is the largest genus of tree-like daisies regionally (~12 species).

The largest is the widespread **Lowveld vernonia** (*Vernonia colorata*), found from northern KwaZulu-Natal and Swaziland through Mozambique and into Zimbabwe. It is a bushveld and scrub species, occurring along streams and on forest edges. The leaves are wavy and quilted, 60–200 mm long, dark green and sandpapery above, paler and woolly below, with a tapering base and apex. The edges are entire to very finely toothed.

Tarchonanthus has three species, all with tough, thickish, strongly bicoloured leaves:

Coastal camphor-bush (*T. littoralis*) ranges in size from a shrub to a small tree and occurs along the coast. The leaves are greyish-green and minutely puckered above, whitish and felt-like below, with entire to finely toothed edges. When crushed, the leaves are aromatic. It is very similar to the widespread Bushveld camphor-bush (*T. camphoratus*), not shown here.

BW

Lowveld vernonia inflorescences. The individual florets are well separated from each other.

HFG

Lowveld vernonias have large leaves. The young central leaves are covered in dense white hairs that disappear with age.

The under-surface of a **Coastal camphor-bush** leaf has a thick covering of matted hair. Note the rolled margins with occasional smooth green bumps.

Coastal camphor-bushes have woolly fruits. ***Inset:*** View of the upper-surface of the leaf. From above the secondary veins are indented, whereas from below there are clear indentations between the veins.

Trident camphor-bushes (*T. trilobus*) have thick leathery leaves that are dark green and roughly corrugated above with indented venation, and whitish below. Two varieties occur, one with trident-shaped leaf apices, and the other with rounded apices. Trident camphor-bushes occur in bushveld habitat, usually at rocky sites and in dry forest, from about East London to Swaziland and into North West and Limpopo provinces, with outliers in northeastern Zimbabwe.

Oldenburgia is a monospecific genus: **Donkey ears** (*O. grandis*) have a restricted distribution on the grass-covered sandstone hills around Grahamstown. These small trees are unmistakable because of their large upright leaves (100–300 mm), which are tough and quilted above, pale cream and woolly below.

EvJ

Donkey ears have very large flowering heads.

EvJ

Donkey ears showing the characteristic leaves and a cluster of flowering heads.

The **Trident camphor-bush** has a variety of leaf forms: this specimen has rounded leaf apices.

This **Trident camphor-bush** is the variety that has trident-shaped leaf apices.

Notes

- The daisy 'flower' is actually a number of small flowers all crowed together on a flat disc (called a capitulum). There are two kinds of flower structures on the capitulum: tiny flowers with regular petals making a tube or trumpet shape that are called disc florets, and ray florets where some of the petals are much longer. Ray florets make up the showy part of the 'flowers' in many daisy species.
- Some species in the family have only disc florets (many of the trees), some have only ray florets, and some have disc florets in the centre of the 'flower' with one or several rows of ray florets around the outside.

Cabbage-tree Family

Araliaceae

~250 spp. globally; ~11 spp. regionally, ~13 spp. of tree

The trees in this family have the following distinguishing characteristics:

- ✓ trees are generally sparsely branched
- ✓ leaves clustered in apical balls
- ✓ leaves mostly compound, sometimes intricately so (>300 mm long)
- ✓ inflorescence usually protrudes above the leaf ball
- ✓ flowers small (<15 mm), pale cream to green, usually in tight spikes
- ✓ fruits thinly fleshy (~3 mm), turning purplish when ripe

There is one species of *Schefflera* in the region, the **African schefflera** (*S. umbellifera*), which is a large coastal forest tree that also occurs on forest edges along the escarpment and into the tropics.

One species of cabbage-tree has simple leaves. This is the **Simple-leaved cabbage-tree** (*Cussonia natalensis*), a small, thickset bushveld species. It is uncommon, occurring from KwaZulu-Natal into Zimbabwe.

One species, the **Octopus cabbage-tree** (*C. arborea*), has digitally compound leaves. It is medium-sized and occurs in miombo bushveld, often on rocky sites.

The stocky **Mountain cabbage-tree** (*C. paniculata*) has distinctive blue-green leaves and occurs on rocky outcrops, mostly in grassland and bushveld habitat in the Eastern Cape.

African scheffleras are large trees. They hold their flowers well above the canopy. ***Inset:*** The leaves are palmately compound and the leaflets have a wavy entire margin.

BW

Octopus cabbage-trees are named for their tentacle-like spicate inflorescences.

BW

The **Simple-leaved cabbage-tree** has thin inflorescence spikes and deeply lobed serrate leaves.

EvJ

A **Mountain cabbage-tree** showing the blackish bark and bluish leaves. ***Inset:*** All cabbage-trees produce a new terminal flush of leaves each year.

The remaining species have leaves that are characteristically twice-palmate.

The **Gamtoos cabbage-tree** (*C. gamtoosensis*) has the least intricately divided leaves. This small bushveld tree is confined to the Eastern Cape. It has very tough, leathery, blue-green leaves.

Two of the largest cabbage-trees are the **Round-headed cabbage-tree** (*C. sphaerocephala*), which is a very tall forest tree in South Africa, and the **Bushveld cabbage-tree** (*C. spicata*), which can be a thickset bushveld tree or a large tree on forest edges. The two species may be confused and are best distinguished when in flower and fruit.

Round-headed cabbage-trees bear leaves in terminal balls. ***Inset:*** Note that the flowering spikes tend to be spherical and not elongate as in the Bushveld cabbage-tree.

Both the **Bushveld** and the **Round-headed cabbage-tree** have complex palmately compound leaves on long petioles.

The young inflorescence spikes of a **Bushveld cabbage-tree** are elongate.

HFG

A **Gamtoos cabbage-tree** bearing inflorescences. Note the characteristic upright leaves.

EvJ

Inflorescences of a **Gamtoos cabbage-tree**. ***Inset:*** The leaves are remarkably tough and have quite sharp spiky tips.

Notes

- Cabbage-trees have traditionally not been cleared from croplands because of their supposed magical properties. Therefore, they can be more conspicuous than they would otherwise be.
- Because of the apical leaf ball, many species of cabbage-tree are prominent. When the wind blows, their large leaves wave wildly on the long leaf stalks.
- Although seemingly woody, the trunks and branches of members of this family are in fact made of tightly packed fibres (similar to those of the African baobab).

Glossary

alternate describing the positioning of leaves that occur singly at different points on the twig (5).

anther pollen-bearing body (26).

apical peg small, bluntly pointed outgrowth at the apical end of a bushwillow (*Combretum*) fruit.

aril outer covering or appendage attached to a seed, often brightly coloured and with a different texture, usually serving as an aid to dispersal.

asymmetric of a leaf in which the two parts on either side of the mid-vein have different dimensions and shapes (24).

attenuate/acuminate of a leaf that tapers to a long point (19).

axillary bud bud occurring where the petiole is attached to the stem (3).

bipinnate, bipinnately compound twice divided; of a compound leaf with leaflets that divide a second time into smaller leaflets (15).

buttress/buttressed woody supporting structures at the base of a tree trunk.

calyx cup-shaped, generally green, outer floral parts comprised of individual sepals; protects the flower bud (26).

catkin spike-like inflorescence typically seen in willows; petals and sepals are not apparent, although scales may be present.

compound of leaves divided into two or more separate leaflets that may be arranged in various ways (9–15).

cone woody, long-lived fruit that may comprise a few or many woody bracts clustered tightly together.

coppice new growth from the base of a tree, often where it has been damaged; leaves on such shoots frequently differ from those on ordinary twigs.

corolla the petals of a flower as a group (26).

deciduous (especially of leaves) falling at the end of a season.

decussate opposite leaf arrangement in which alternate pairs are at right angles to each other.

dehiscent splitting open; of a dry fruit that opens to release seeds.

deltoid roughly triangular in shape.

digitate radiating leaflet arrangement, like fingers on a hand; see *palmate* (12).

drip-tip spout-like, elongate extension of a leaf apex (18).

elliptic oval in outline; wide in the middle with narrower ends (21).

entire of a leaf margin that lacks serrations (16).

exfoliolate peel off in layers or flakes.

exserted extending above, e.g. describing anthers that project over the corolla or floral tube.

gall unnatural growth caused by some external agent such as a virus or insect larva.

globose globe-like in shape.

gynophore long basal stalk that bears an ovary that is not nested in the base of the flower – characteristic of the caper family (Capparaceae).

heterogeneous unrelated, different from one another.

imparipinnate of pinnately compound leaves that have an unequal number of leaflets (13).

indehiscent not splitting open; of dry fruits that stay closed, thus retaining the seeds.

inflorescence flowering structure that consists of more than one flower.

internode part of a stem or twig between two nodes.

interpetiolar between petioles; of the stipules of opposite leaves when they connect one petiole base with the opposite one (see photo opposite).

intrapetiolar going from one side of the base of the petiole to the other side of the same petiole, forming a tiny envelope in the leaf axil, between the petiole base and the twig – occurs rarely.

knee-root breathing roots of the Black mangrove (*Bruguiera gymnorrhiza*) that extend above ground, bend and go straight back into the ground.

lanceolate lance-shaped; widest about one-third from the base and pointed at both ends (25).

leaflet one segment/division of a compound leaf (9).

lenticel small, corky, raised area on a twig, usually of a different colour and texture; needed for gaseous exchange.

liana woody climber.

lobe deeply divided, usually rounded, part of a leaf, generally with an entire margin (22, 23).

marginal teeth small, tooth-like, often spiky projections along the margin or edge of a leaf (17).

midrib main vein of a leaf; may be in the middle or to one side, in which case the two sides of the leaf will be unequal in area and the leaf will be asymmetric (1).

monospecific of a genus that comprises just one species.

mucro short and sometimes sharp extension of the midrib beyond the leaf apex (20).

naturalised of an introduced species now growing in indigenous vegetation like a native.

node twig joint where a leaf is attached; sometimes appears as a slight bump.

ovoid three-dimensional egg-shape.

palmate arrangement of the leaflets in a compound leaf that resembles fingers on a hand; see *digitate* (12).

Simple leaves

1

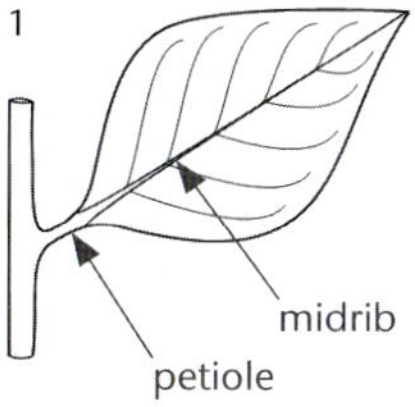

2

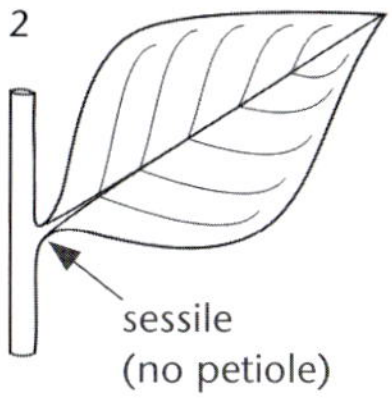

3

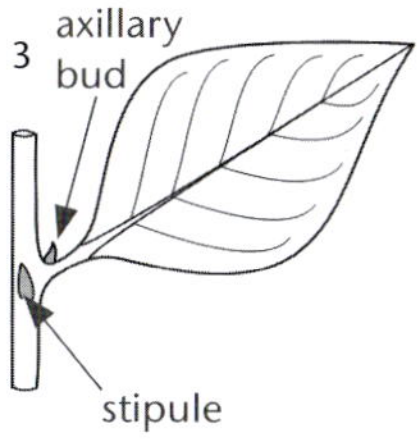

4

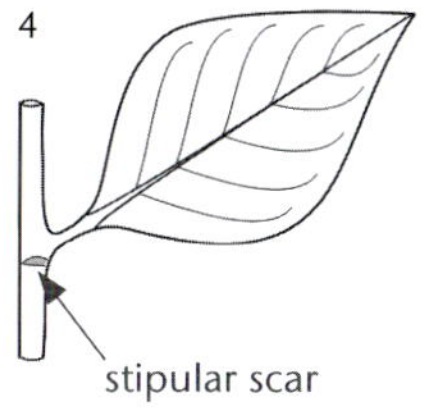

Leaf arrangements

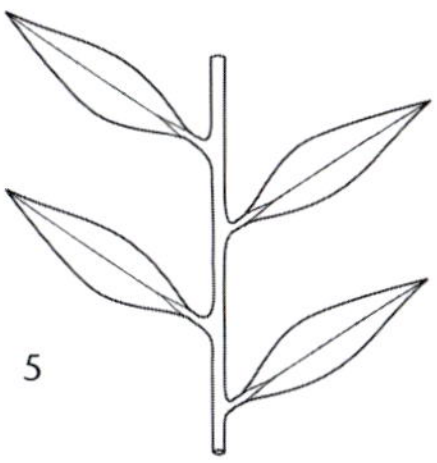

5

simple alternate

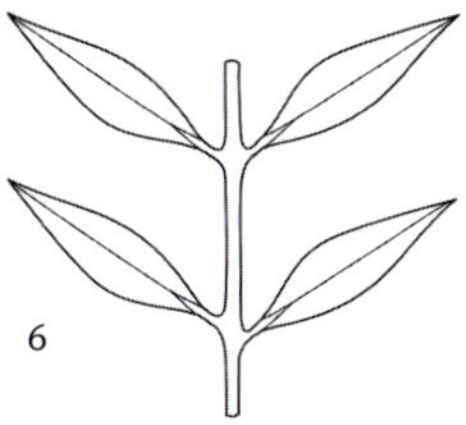

6

simple opposite

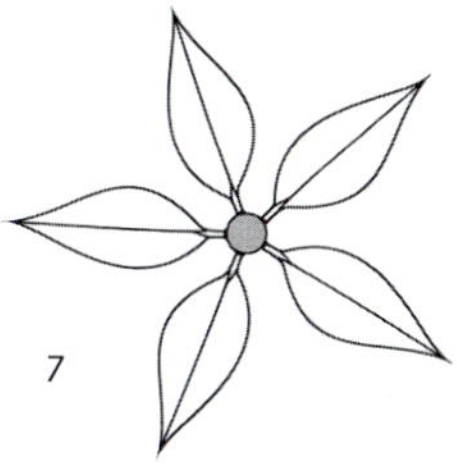

7

whorled

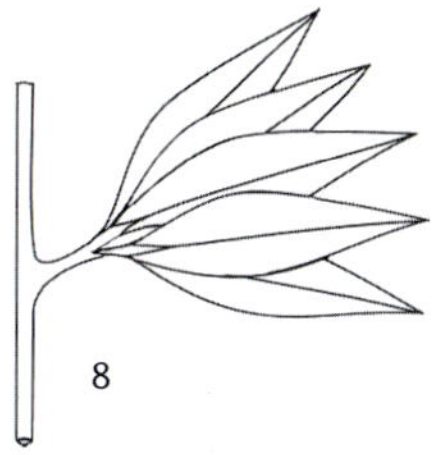

8

tufted

Compound leaves

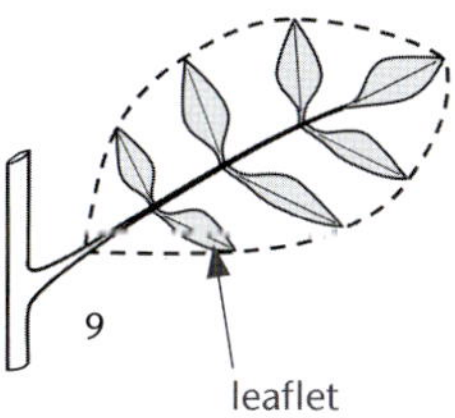

9

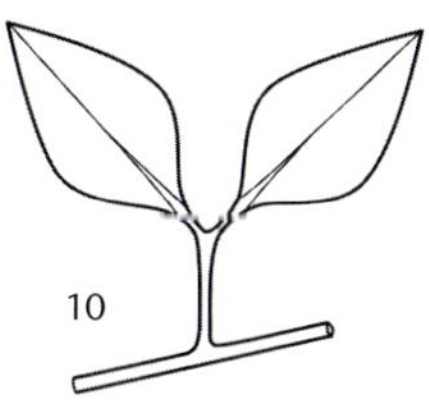

10

bifoliolate

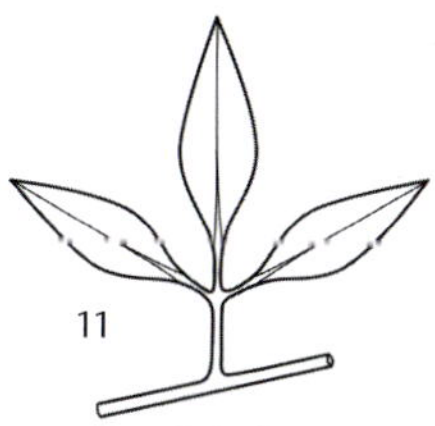

11

trifoliolate

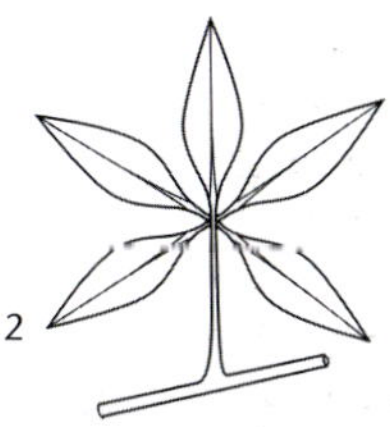

12

digitate/palmate

13

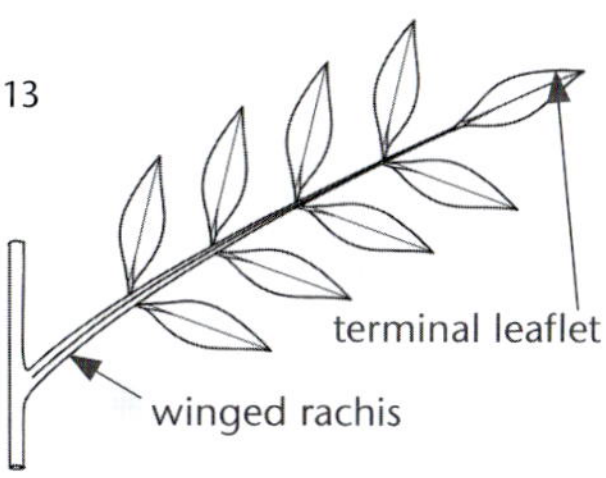

imparipinnate

Members of the Rubiaceae have simple, opposite leaves with entire margins and interpetiolar stipules that are usually conspicuous. Here the stipule is not only conspicuous, but also large – it sheaths the twig, joining the petiole bases of the leaves.

14

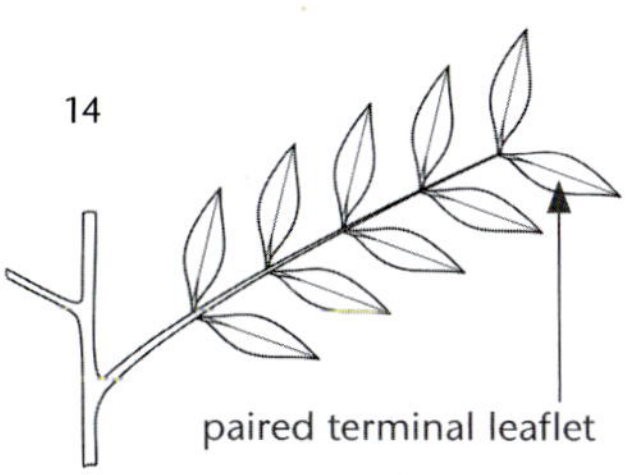

paripinnate

15

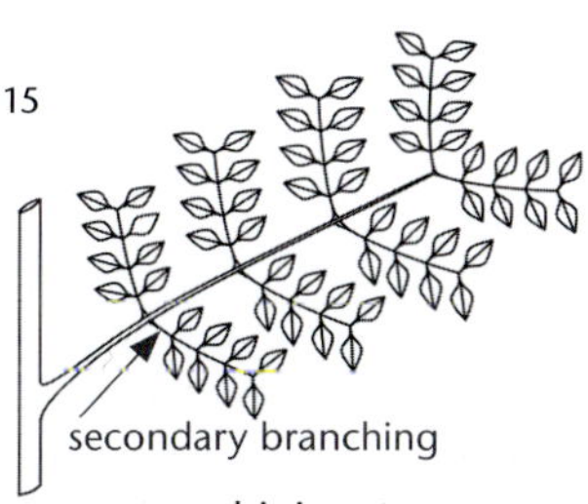

bipinnate

paripinnate of pinnately compound leaves that have an equal number of leaflets (14).
petiole leaf stalk (1).
pinnate, pinnately compound of leaves that are once-divided with four or more leaflets that may be alternate or opposite on the rachis and that may be imparipinnate (i.e. an odd number of leaflets and a terminal leaflet) or paripinnate (i.e. an even number of leaflets and a final leaflet pair) (9, 13, 14).
pistil female flower organ that bears the ovules or seeds in the ovary, style and stigma (26).
pliable flexible or bendable; not rigid.
primary venation see *venation*.
prop-root specialised root that grows from a tree trunk above the ground and assists in propping up the tree; an adaptation of some species, like certain mangroves, that grow in soft substrates.
pulvinus a swollen petiole base that can usually lose or retain water, allowing the leaf to droop or stand firm for various reasons (leaves of the exotic Sensitive mimosas (*Mimosa pudica*), for instance, droop on contact to make them look unpalatable).
pustule a cluster of lenticels; appears as a large, generally raised, rough, brownish area.
rachis central leaf stalk of a compound leaf; like the midrib of a simple leaf; provides a support structure for the leaflets and may be winged in some species (13).
rank, two-ranked a line or row; leaves that are two-ranked are arranged in two rows so that the leaves are alternate on opposite sides of the twig in the same plane (also referred to as distichous).
recurved bent or arched backwards.
reticulum fine network of veins in a leaf.
riparian of a river course or bank, or pertaining to seasonal drainage lines.
scandent of a plant that is not strictly a climber, but leans on other plants for support; a weak tree.
secondary venation see *venation*.
serrate saw-like, usually with the teeth pointing forwards (towards the leaf apex) (17).
sessile lacking a stalk; often of a leaf with a base that is attached directly to the twig (2).
simple undivided; of a leaf with only a single blade (1).
spicate spike-like; of an inflorescence that is unbranched, elongate and has sessile flowers.
spinescent having spines; ending in a sharp, woody point.
stamen male part of the flower comprising a filament (stalk) and an anther (the pollen container) (26).
stellate star-like.
stipular scar the scar formed once the stipule has fallen off (4) (see also photo opposite).
stipulate having stipules.
stipule appendage at the base of a petiole that may be tiny, large or even leafy; can be shed early or may persist for some time; stipules in many species are the protective bracts that cover and protect the axillary bud (3).
sub-woody lacking lignin; not comprised of true woody tissue.
sun-leaves leaves that grow in full sunlight, usually at the top of the canopy.
tertiary venation see *venation*.
trifoliolate of a compound leaf with three leaflets (11).
truncheon a short living branch or twig that is cut to propagate that species.
venation of the arrangement of the veins in a leaf: the primary vein is the mid-vein running up the centre of a simple leaf; secondary veins diverge off the mid-vein towards the margin and these branch again and again forming tertiary veins. In some plants there can be more than one prominent basal vein (16).
whorl three or more leaves that arise at one place/point on the twig (7).
wing flat, usually thin, sometimes papery, appendage or extension on a petiole, rachis, or fruit (see also *rachis*).

The leaves of the **Quiver-tree aloe** are spirally arranged and are clustered apically.

Leaf margins

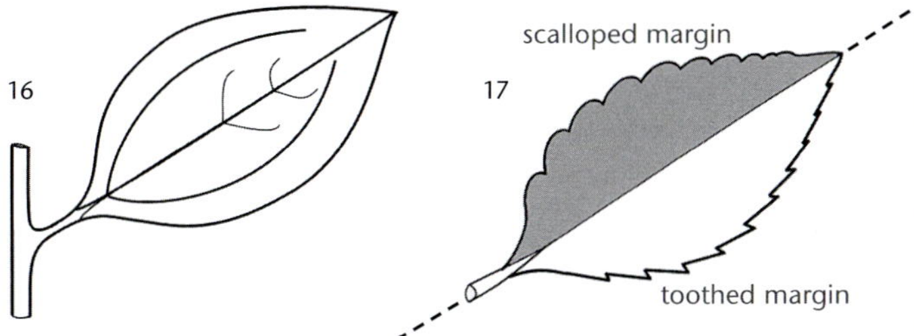

16 entire/smooth

17 scalloped; serrate

The African red-alder or Butter spoon (*Cunonia capensis*) is known for its large interpetiolar stipules, which cover and protect the bud (1). They fall as the leaves unfurl and mature, leaving a conspicuous scar (2).

Leaf apices

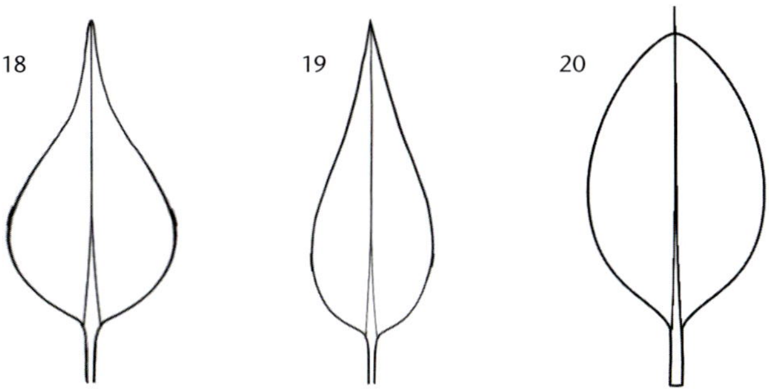

18 drip-tip

19 attenuate tip

20 mucronate tip

Leaf shapes

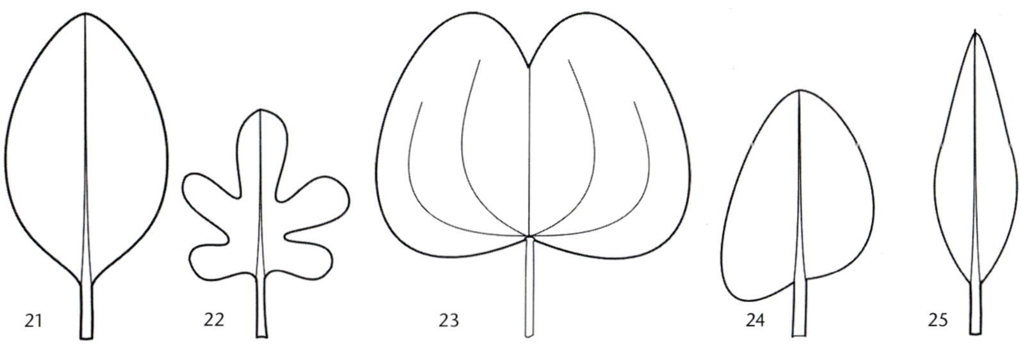

21 elliptic

22 lobed

23 bilobed

24 asymmetric

25 lancecolate

Floral structure

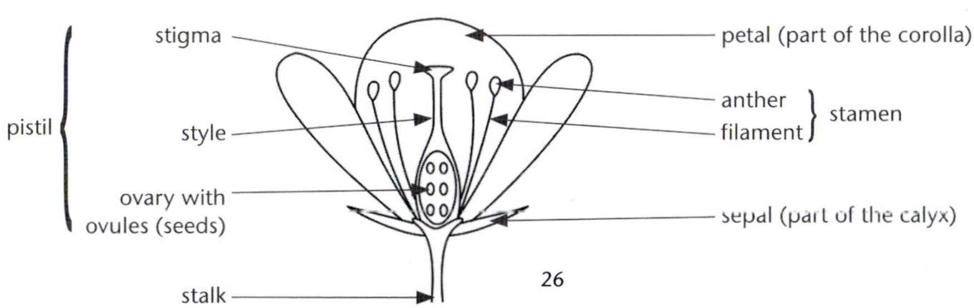

26

Acknowledgements

Trees are my first and enduring love, so my heartfelt thanks go to Pippa Parker for inviting me to write this book. Then to all of the Struik team my most sincere gratitude, especially Emily Bowles for her meticulous, relentless and insightful editorial inputs. And to Dr John Manning for suggesting that I follow the latest classification of plants, making this the first guide to do so.

The identification of trees is a challenge for beginners, so from the start I knew that I had to have excellent photographs of specific diagnostic features for this book. Therefore, without the unstinting and incredibly generous assistance of all the photographers who came to my aid, often taking and re-taking photographs until they had the precise image I required, this task would have been impossible. Tree lovers everywhere owe all of you very special people a huge debt of gratitude for your generous support and love of plants. (Please see the list of contributing photographers that follows. Each photograph is individually credited in the text.) A special word of thanks goes to a new friend, Ted Woods, an amateur tree enthusiast, who has generously shared not only his photographs but also his tree identification insights and sketches for the glossary.

Finally this book would not have been possible without the help and support of my family and many friends, among them Ernst van Jaarsveld and Mervyn Lötter, who not only provided photographs but also read the final text. To all of you, and particularly my wife Alice for her continual support and my grandson Joshua Khoury for the poem that follows, a huge and most sincere thank you.

Poetree

They are home to all
Rooted to the spot
Endlessly interesting
Exotic and beautiful
Swaying elegantly in the breeze

I've got treez – identify them pleaz!!!!

Josh Khoury, age 9

List of photographers

The following is a key to the abbreviations used for photographers' names. The number of photographs contributed by each individual is indicated in brackets.

AG Andy Gubb (1)
AJ André Joubert (3)
AM Andy Moore (1)
AS Adam Shuttleworth (24)

BC Barbara Curtis (3)
BP Barry Porter (10)
BT Brendon Thorpe (1)
BW Bart Wursten (47)

CG Coert Geldenhuys (1)
CS Cody Sehl (1)
CV Carl Vernon (14)

DP Darrel Plowes (3)

EvJ Ernst van Jaarsveld (47)

GG Graham Grieve (11)
GN Geoff Nichols (19)

HFG Hugh F Glen (32)

JB Jan Burring (32)
JD John Donaldson (2)
J-D John Dransfield (1)
JE Jenny Eldridge (1)
JEB John Burrows (2)

LL Linda Loffler (15)

MH Mark Hyde (2)
ML Mervyn Lötter (9)

NC Neil Crouch (7)

RB Richard Boon (5)

TA Tony Abbott (7)
TC Tony Cunningham (12)
TP Tim Peatling (1)
TW Ted Woods (12)

WS Wessel Swanepoel (4)
WT Wayne Twine (2)

Index